Saved Twice

By Gail Wood

Copyright © 2009 by Gail Wood

Saved Twice
by Gail Wood

Printed in the United States of America

ISBN 9781615794348

All rights reserved solely by the author. The author guarantees all contents are original and do not infringe upon the legal rights of any other person or work. No part of this book may be reproduced in any form without the permission of the author. The views expressed in this book are not necessarily those of the publisher.

www.xulonpress.com

Contents

Introduction vii
1 – Trapped With No Air 9
2 – Out Of Hope 16
3 – A Fall From Fame 22
4 – Don't Cut It Off 27
5 – Running Scared 33
6 – Surviving An Avalanche 39
7 – Dead On Arrival 45
8 – A Miraculous Comeback 51
9 – A Heart For God 58
10 – Eyes On The Goal 64
11 – Running From Danger 69
12 – Graduation, Cancer and Chemo 76
13 – A Race Against Death 83

Introduction

෧෪

The thirteen people in this book, from the all-star first baseman to the Pac-10 coach of the year to the 16-year-old girl who survives after being held under water 45 minutes in a canoe accident, share some common traits. As athletes, they have inspired.

Whether it was when John Olerud faced a 3-2 count with the go-ahead run on second, or when Brian Sternberg arched over the bar to set another world pole vault record, or when Marty Tadman intercepted a pass and returned it for a touchdown, they have inspired us with their athletic talent.

But in this book each of them inspires us with their Christian faith. With their courage in the face of death. With their commitment to God.

Each has been saved twice. First, as Christians they were saved by grace. Second, they were saved from a life-threatening situation. They've been saved from physical danger and saved from their sins.

The people in this book, from a mountain-climbing guide who is swept away by an avalanche to a Pac-10 guard whose heart stopped, putting in motion a race to save her life, share their inspirational stories about overcoming accidents, injuries or dangerous moments in their lives. With their dramatic storyline as a backdrop, they share how God is there in the good and bad times. They share about the power of prayer.

vii

Saved Twice

About facing death. And about survival. Their real-life dramas will encourage your faith.

We all love a comeback victory. These stories are about the best comebacks ever. They bring hope and inspiration.

Because of a press pass I've covered the Super Bowl, the NBA finals, the NCAA finals, the AL championship series and the Rose Bowl. I've talked with the game's biggest names—Michael Jordan, Shawn Alexander, Ken Griffey Jr. I've watched the biggest moments in sports. The biggest games. But the stories in the following pages trump all those moments.

I'm an award-winning sportswriter who has written for over sixty newspapers and magazines. The Seattle Times presented me a Blethen Memorial Award for feature writing. Gannett named me columnist of the year. I've written for USA Today, Seattle Times, Athlon Sports, Guideposts, Charisma and numerous other publications.

Chapter 1

Trapped With No Air

§§

Frantically, Carly Boohm pushed on the side of the canoe to free her leg.

Trapped underwater in a river, her leg was pinched by the side of the canoe that had collapsed after slamming into a bridge.

Unable to pull free, Carly, her lungs aching for air, poked her hand above the water and waved for help.

Someone on shore saw her hand and quickly dialed 911 and a dramatic rescue began.

A day that was nearly Carly's last started on a chilly April morning. She and seven friends from her church in the small logging town of Tenino, Washington, packed into a white van early one Saturday morning and headed across the mountain pass to the Wenatchee River in eastern Washington. They were going to take part in the Ridge-to-River Relay, a race that begins with snow skiing and ends with canoeing down the Wenatchee River. Thousands of racers come each year to this picturesque valley dotted with tall pine trees and rugged snow-capped Cascade Mountains as a backdrop.

Except Carly wasn't going to race. She was simply going to drive, moving canoes and racers a few miles along the course. She was sixteen. Driving was still an adventure.

9

Saved Twice

Before going, Carly received a word of advice.

"Remember to stay out of the river," Carly's mother, Barbara, said for the umpteenth time before dropping her daughter off that morning.

Carly didn't need any reminders. A friend of her parents had drowned in the Wenatchee River the year before.

But shortly after completing the four-hour drive to Wenatchee and just after they pulled into a scenic park along the Wenatchee River, someone said, "Come on. Let's go canoeing."

They still had a few hours before the race actually began. Not wanting to be left out, Carly phoned her mother.

"Everybody's doing it," Carly pleaded.

Reluctantly her mother consented.

"Be careful," her mother said before hanging up.

With one foot in the canoe and the other on the sandy beach, Reuben Andrews shoved off from shore, his back leg dangling briefly. The fourteen-foot aluminum canoe holding three friends moved briskly down the choppy Wenatchee River.

"Here we go," Reuben shouted as he cut a deep stroke with his paddle, his voice muffled by the roar of the river.

Carly sat in the middle, gripping the sides of the canoe. In the bow, Marya Denzer, Carly's classmate and best friend, paddled.

Carly had never been in a canoe. Neither had Reuben and Marya. But all three carefully stepped into a fourteen-foot aluminum canoe and pushed off into the swift waters. Because of unusually high rainfall and melting snow the river was rushing at about seven-thousand cubic feet per second, the highest rate in years.

They hadn't gone more than a few blocks when the canoe overturned, dumping the three friends into the snow-fed waters and sweeping them down river. They bobbed like

10

Saved Twice

corks in the dark, choppy waters as they floated to a little sandy island. Somehow, Reuben pushed the canoe to shore.

"I don't want to get back into that canoe," Carly protested, shivering with cold.

All she was wearing was a lightweight, blue-colored pullover shirt, a yellow lifejacket and shorts. Her long brown hair soaked, Carly was freezing. And scared.

But they still needed to get to the other side of the river.

"Come on, Carly," Reuben insisted.

He pointed to a sandy beach down river just past the Sleepy Hollow Bridge. It was their only escape. They didn't want to swim to shore in such swift waters. Reluctantly, Carly climbed back into the canoe. Reuben and Marya again paddled. As they approached the narrow, two-lane bridge, the canoe shifted broadside and headed toward a pillar.

"Paddle harder!" Reuben shouted.

But the swift waters sucked the canoe toward the bridge support. Reuben dropped his paddle and reached to push off the pillar. The canoe slammed into the pillar, throwing Reuben and Marya into the choppy water. They quickly swam to shore and safety.

Carly wasn't as fortunate. The tremendous pressure of the river collapsed a side of the canoe, pinching tightly onto Carly's leg, trapping her. She was just three feet under the surface in water that was about thirty feet deep at the bridge. Unable to pull free, her lungs ached for air.

One minute passed. Two minutes passed. Someone from the shore saw Carly's hand frantically waving above the water and dialed 911 on a cell phone. It was 2:49 in the afternoon.

Just then Everett Gahringer, a volunteer policeman patrolling the river in his fifteen-foot aluminum boat, spotted Carly's upraised hand. He revved his one-100-horsepower motor and quickly pulled next to the overturned canoe that was stuck against the bridge. He could see Carly under the water, struggling.

As Everett fought to hold his boat still, a friend of his onboard reached toward Carly. Their hands nearly touched.

Three minutes passed. Carly's hand went limp. She was drowning.

"Please, God, save me," Carly prayed. "Don't let me die."

Frantically, Everett tried wrapping a rope around the bow of the canoe that was a few feet underwater. He could see the bottom of the canoe was against the concrete pillar and the side of the canoe had pinched down onto Carly's leg. She had no air pocket to breathe from.

For several minutes Everett bucked the swift current, his motor roaring above the rushing river. He circled the canoe four times, tugging at the rope in hope of jarring Carly free. But it was useless. He feared his boat would be swamped or flipped.

Ten minutes passed.

Three men in the sheriff's V8 inboard jet-engine boat arrived and took over the rescue. They tried pulling the canoe free with a rope. But again it was futile. The river was too powerful.

Fifteen minutes passed. Twenty minutes.

Not knowing what to do Everett went to shore, thinking the rescue was over.

"At that point I thought it was just a recovery," Everett said. "I didn't think there was any chance of saving her."

It was now about 3:15. Carly had been underwater for 26 minutes. Everyone thought it was too late to save her. Everyone except Shawn Ballard, one of the medics on the scene. He knew the icy waters slowed Carly's body functions, extending her chance of surviving without air. On this day, water temperatures were just above freezing.

Saved Twice

"Let's try again," Shawn yelled through cupped hands, setting into action another rescue attempt. "We've got until 3:30."

Just then a county fire truck rolled onto the bridge. A hole was punched through the bow of the canoe, and a cable was looped through it. The tires of the fire truck bounced under the strain of the winch, which was capable of pulling 30,000 pounds. Slowly the canoe began to rise. With the winch straining and the canoe halfway out of the water, an unconscious Carly popped free. The current swept her down river, her bright-yellow lifejacket keeping her afloat. Everett revved his motor and raced to retrieve her.

"I got to her as quick as I could," he said.

After being underwater for forty-five minutes, Carly was free.

She still wasn't breathing. Her heart had stopped. But now at least she had a chance.

Inside the ambulance Shawn threaded a tube into Carly's windpipe, and Carla Render squeezed a ball to push air into Carly's lungs. Carla's sister had drowned in a car accident in Idaho, and she was praying Carly would be saved. Shawn then used a defibrillator to start Carly's heart. It stopped, started and stopped again. Each time he used shock pads to jolt her heart back to life. He injected epinephrine directly into her heart. Her heart briefly increased five beats a minute to fifty. All this time he was praying, "God, please save this girl."

Carly's body temperature was seventy-two degrees when she arrived at the hospital. If she lived, doctors feared Carly would be little more than a vegetable because her brain had gone so long without air. They gave her a two-percent chance of living. In a risky move doctors used a kidney dialysis machine to warm Carly's blood.

Four days after nearly drowning, Carly slowly raised her arm and waved to her mom, who was sitting by her

Saved Twice

hospital bed. It was a miracle. Carly, Barbara's only child, was alive.

"The doctors have used the word miracle over and over again," her mother said.

But Carly's recovery was far from over. The straight-A student had to relearn how to walk and talk. Reading a third-grader's book was a struggle. Her mother would ask, "What does a cat say?" Carly would respond, "Meow."

After Carly was released from the hospital, her father, Phil, walked around the high school track in their hometown with her, sometimes pulling her along, saying, "Come on, Carly. You can do this."

At first it took twenty minutes to go around the track once. She'd resist, sometimes slugging her dad. But he insisted.

"Okay, Carly, are you going to walk today, or am I going to drag you?" her dad would ask.

Carly, who ran hurdles in track, played soccer and was a cheerleader, spent two-and-a-half months in the hospital. She went to physical therapy, occupational therapy and speech therapy while she attended a community college. She's appeared on "Dateline" and "The Today Show," sharing her rescue and her Christian faith.

"We feel that God has given Carly back to us," her dad said. "She's an answer to prayer. There is no doubt God has played an important role in all of this. People don't stay underwater 45 minutes and survive."

On the day after Carly's accident 150 people held a prayer meeting at her church in Tenino.

"The way I tell the story is man had quit twenty-five minutes into Carly's rescue," Phil said. "Shawn Ballard refused to quit. God was speaking through Shawn when he told everyone to get back into the water. God's hand was in the rescue the whole way. People throughout the rescue were Christians praying."

Saved Twice

Carly sometimes wonders, "Why me, God?" But she knows God is there in good and bad times.

"I'm a miracle. I know that. And I am thankful," Carly said.

At a Christmas tree lighting ceremony at the state capitol, then-governor Gary Locke presented Carly with an award and called her the "state's miracle."

So some good has come out of a horrible experience.

"I've had a chance to tell other people about God's forgiveness and love," Carly said. "My parents know God saved me not once but twice."

Imagine forgetting how to walk. How to hold a pencil. How to read. Imagine being trapped underwater in a rushing river. Imagine being dead. Then, only after a miraculous rescue, alive. This is Carly's story.

She was helpless and hopeless. She was trapped. Her parents say her rescue in the river that day was no less amazing than her rescue and forgiveness from sin by Jesus' death on the cross. Carly was saved twice.

"Carly loves God with all her heart," her father said. "She's always brought as many people as she could to church. That's why she's alive. God is going to use her some more."

Chapter 2

Out of Hope

§♭

Alone on a California ocean beach, eighteen-year-old Marty Tadman, a high school All-American defensive back, agonized about his past and his future.

With tears streaming down his cheeks, Marty came face-to-face with a troubling truth. Everything in his life meant nothing to him.

Not the recruiting letters from USC, Notre Dame, Arizona and Boise State. Not the trophy for being named the Orange County Player of the Year by the Los Angeles Times. And not all the friends he partied with until late into the night every weekend.

"I started looking at what I had been doing the past five years of my life," Marty said. "It was all pointless stuff. I realized I had no idea who I was. I was worthless. A no one. I started crying, screaming. I realized I was a bad person."

To everyone else he had it all. He was a football sensation, a classroom whiz and the most popular kid in his school. But on this Friday night in April 2004, on the beach in San Clemente, not far from his high school in Mission Viejo, California, where everyone knew him as the football

Saved Twice

star with the good looks and the good grades, Marty was filled with despair.

"I thought of suicide. I just wanted to end my life," Marty said.

In desperation he cried out to God.

"I said, 'God, if You are here, prove it to me because I think I'm done with this life,'" Marty said. "After I said that, I felt God's presence."

The next day Marty asked his mother for a Bible. It was an odd request. He was raised Jewish.

"I'd never seen a Bible before," Marty said. "Never read one before. I was a Jewish kid. I didn't really like Christian people."

His mother found a Bible, a small New Testament, distributed by the Gideons.

"I read the first six chapters of Matthew," he said. "After I read the Lord's Prayer I was convinced this was it. This was what I wanted to do. This was what I believed in. I believed Jesus was real. I believed everything He said was real. I said I wanted to live for Him."

Tadman the party man suddenly became Tadman the Bible man.

He became Boise State's free safety, an all-American and a mid-round NFL draft pick. Every Tuesday he led an on-campus Bible study he started, drawing as many as sixty students. He also helped lead a youth group at Eagle Christian Church, sharing his faith and testimony at churches throughout the Northwest during the off-season.

"I want to go into the ministry full-time when my football days are done," he said.

At Boise State's home games Bronco fans are asked to wear blue or orange, the school's colors. But several hundred fans showed up each game wearing black "Madman Tadman" T-shirts. On the back is Galatians 2, with a big 20, his jersey

Saved Twice

number. The scripture—"So it is no longer I who live, but it is Christ who lives in me"—is something he lives by.

Marty thrives on pickoffs and prayers. With twelve interceptions the speedy 5'11" safety came into his senior season with the most career interceptions among active NCAA players. As a junior he picked off two passes in the Fiesta Bowl, returning one interception twenty-seven yards for a touchdown in Boise State's thrilling 43-42 overtime win against Oklahoma.

He is convinced if he hadn't become a Christian he wouldn't have played college football. He's not sure he'd even be alive.

"I had friends who were killed living the same way I did," Marty said.

At thirteen he began smoking marijuana and drinking alcohol. At fifteen he began using cocaine. At sixteen he began selling drugs, sometimes making as much as a thousand dollars in a month.

"My life at sixteen was going to clubs every day, going to parties every day, going to bars every day, trying to get as many girls as I could," Marty said.

At seventeen he was caught by the police with drugs, resulting in misdemeanor charges. It scared him. But still he made such a poor impression at his recruiting visit to Boise State in January 2004 the coaches nearly withdrew a scholarship offer.

Desperate, Marty made his life-changing discovery alone on the California beach. It wasn't at a church or a response to a television evangelist's prompting. It was out of a hunger for something more in life.

"Marty wouldn't say his conversion was a Saul experience on the way to Damascus," said Steve Crane, Marty's pastor at Eagle Christian Church in Eagle, Idaho. "But he would say he knew he had to make a change."

"Nobody really knew me," Marty said.

Saved Twice

Recruiters from USC, Notre Dame and Boise State knew him as a high school All-American, a two-way starter with the knack for making big plays. In high school he played wide receiver, quarterback and defensive back and returned punts.

Friends knew him as the wild partier. His parents—his mother a private investigator and his father a businessman—knew him as a good student, a good athlete and a good kid.

"He was a very good actor," his mother, Joey, said.

He was transformed after that night on the ocean beach, a night he angrily left a party because of a fight. After that encounter with God he stopped doing drugs, stopped partying and stopped womanizing. His high school friends were shocked by the change.

"I saw a complete change in him," said Nicole Marty, his high school girlfriend and now his wife.

"I found a drug more powerful, a party more fun, in God," Marty said. "He showed me true happiness."

Now he calls himself a "walking evangelism cube." His arms are covered with tattoos, including Scripture verses on salvation and drawings of Jesus. It's the gospel message in tattoo form.

"It's a great outreach toward the world," he said. "Not a day goes by that someone doesn't ask about my tattoos."

It's taken fifty-five hours for a Christian friend to do all the tattoos on both of his arms, from his shoulders to his wrists. On one of Boise State's games televised on ESPN, the announcers talked about Marty's Christian faith as cameras showed close-ups of his arms.

He is a committed Christian wanting to make a difference. He's a busy volunteer at his church, sharing his testimony, his time and his connection with BSU.

"And it's not just with our church," Crane said. "He's also spoken at high schools, junior high schools and grade schools."

Saved Twice

Marty, a good golfer, was even auctioned off to play in a foursome, raising money for a building project at Eagle Christian. He then surprised Crane when he auctioned off his BSU jersey.

"Players get to keep one jersey a year," Crane said. "He gave his freshman jersey to his parents. He gave this jersey to the church. That's just Marty."

The jersey went for about sixteen thousand dollars.

It's his passion that makes his testimony so powerful. He's been through so much. For several years Crane mentored Marty, meeting with him once a week for instruction and accountability.

After several meetings, Crane worried Marty wasn't taking the sessions seriously.

"The first couple of times we met I was really disappointed because he didn't write anything down. He never took notes."

Finally, Crane put Marty on the spot.

"I said, 'Marty, I want you to share with me what I've been sharing with you the last couple of weeks,'" Crane said."And verbatim he gave it right back to me. He has a phenomenal mind, as well as Christian character. He's a very smart guy."

Boise State coach Chris Peterson has called Marty "the smartest guy in college football."

Marty's conversion story from drugs to Christ has drawn national attention, told in magazines, newspapers and web sites.

"He's always giving his testimony," Crane said.

"I see football as a platform," Marty said. "It's my opportunity to share my faith."

The national attention, his success on the football field and even the attention and admiration inside his church haven't inflated his ego. A Boise State graduate went so far as to name his child, Marty Tadman Nettles. But his celeb-

20

Saved Twice

rity status hasn't changed how he sees himself—a forgiven sinner.

"You won't see Marty getting all puffed up," Crane said. "It's more, come on—I'm just a football player. He'll say on the scale of things football is really unimportant. He really tries to point people toward Christ. He gives God the glory."

Marty's commitment to sharing his hope and faith in Jesus is why he's used his arms as a flannel board, telling the gospel's message of salvation. Crane has seen Marty's tattooed message. He shares the same message, but not necessarily the mode of the message.

"Oh, I don't want my sons to get tattoos," he said with a chuckle. "I don't condone tattoos. But Marty is going to reach a group of people I can't."

Marty's insight into despair also helps him empathize and connect with the down and out.

He's the illustrated man with a mission.

"What Marty tries to do is point people toward Christ," Crane said. "He gives God the glory."

Marty Tadman's journey has taken him from drug and alcohol abuse, from a suicidal teen, to a national pedestal as an All-American football player on a nationally ranked team, to leading a Bible study and working in a church. The transformation is like night and day.

"I was ready to end my life," Marty said. "I came to the beach that night with nothing, and I left with everything."

Chapter 3

A Fall From Fame

His world records came so unexpectedly, so suddenly. He was only 19, a sophomore pole vaulter at the University of Washington. He had finished second at his state high school championship just two years earlier.

But during a remarkable three-month span in the spring of 1963 Brian Sternberg broke the world pole vault record three times, his muscular body arching over the bar at record-breaking heights in Philadelphia in April, again in Modesto, California, in May and again in Los Angeles in June. Using a fiberglass pole that had just been introduced, he was the first to attempt 17 feet.

Three meets. Three world records.

His coach predicted he'd be the first to clear 20 feet. The Olympics, less than a year away, were expected to be his showcase.

But on July 2, 1963, three days before heading with the U.S. team to the Soviet Union for a meet, Brian broke his neck working out on a trampoline. Losing his sense of "up and down" while doing a full twist, double-back somersault, Brian landed on his head, paralyzing him from the neck down. He had dislocated a vertebra, injuring his spine as he sustained a C4-C5 spinal injury.

Saved Twice

He lay on the trampoline unable to move. As the trampoline springs continued to bounce him around, he remembers watching his arms and legs flop without his control.

In an instant Brian's remarkable moment on a world stage ended.

Now, almost five decades later, he is still totally dependent on others. He can't walk, can't feed or dress himself.

As a pole vaulter he wowed the world. As a quadriplegic he's inspired it, his Christian faith unbending.

His moment of fame was so fleeting, lasting a year. But his faith in Christ has endured.

"Things didn't go as I expected," the 65-year-old Brian said. "But you have to realize that even when things don't go as you had hoped they would, you can always make the best of it."

Brian's words come slowly. Each one is labored. He pauses for short breaths between words.

His circumstances have changed. But he said the truth of the cross hasn't.

"That's my strength."

He refuses to blame God for his injury. He admits he's angry that he can't do things for himself, simple things like pour himself a glass of juice. He also admits he's been overcome with disappointment, discouragement because his dreams of being an Olympic athlete turned into a nightmare. Yet he can't believe that an accident that turned him into a quadriplegic was a plan of God.

"Some people say God struck me down to better use me," Brian said. "I don't believe that at all. I couldn't believe in a God who would do this. But He's made it possible to use it. Sure, there's a better way to live, but this has been pretty positive."

That outlook has been his cure for bitterness.

His mother, Helen Sternberg, helped care for her son for 40 years before her death. An uncommon bond existed

Saved Twice

between mother and son, a bond nurtured in commitment. And like her son, Helen didn't blame God.

"The only way you could become bitter is if you thought God had done this to you," she said. "We've always maintained that accidents happen. Then, as Brian has said, it's up to you where you turn. You can turn bitter, or you can turn the other way."

Blaming God, she said, misses the point.

"When you attribute everything that happens to God, you don't have room for the enemy.," Helen said. "That's what has sustained us. We feel we're on the right side."

Brian, the youngest of two children and the son of a housing contractor in Seattle, still lives in the basement of his parents' home. Harold Sternberg, Brian's doting father, died fifteen years ago.

Brian was injured before John F. Kennedy was assassinated, before the Beatles were a hit and before man walked on the moon. But Brian Sternberg hasn't been forgotten. He was recently inducted into North America's Pole Vaulters Hall of Fame and flew to Las Vegas for the induction. Not long ago he received a letter from Europe that was simply addressed: Injured pole vaulter. No state, city or zip code was mentioned.

"I'm amazed at how many people remember Brian," his mother said.

After he had experimental surgery in 1997 that helped his condition he received over 5,000 get-well wishes. But most people tend to forget.

Someone who hasn't forgotten is Catherine Palmer, who attended high school with Brian and is now his daytime attendant. For 11 years she has cared for Brian, feeding him, taking him to Washington Husky football, basketball and track events. Interestingly, it's Catherine, a grandmother, who has said she's the one who receives the pick-me-ups when she's down.

Saved Twice

"I look forward to going to work every day," she said. "When I get there I'll ask Brian how he's doing. And sometimes he'll say, 'Better now that you're here.' He's that kind of person."

Catherine has never heard him complain about his condition.

"He's a delight to be with," she said. "I've never met anyone like him."

A typical day for Brian is a movie in the morning, lunch and a nap, and after that he'll e-mail friends, typing out messages with a wand he clinches between his teeth. He talks about everything from the Seattle Mariners to his involvement with the Fellowship of Christian Athletes.

"I'm not a very fast typer," he said. "I'm a slow hunt-and-peck. But I make my way through."

Brian was raised in a Christian home, and his faith has endured the hard times. He admits he has struggled when his prayers for healing were not answered. His problem is answering the question: "Why did this happen?"

"The hard thing is keeping the faith," he said. "But what do you do? You've got to make the most out of what you have."

Leaning on friends, faith and family, Brian learned to accept his condition and its limitations. He realized it was futile to waste energy complaining about something that would not change. He decided early on it was time to make something of who he was.

"Brian has never given up hope," his mother said. "His philosophy is if you can get something good out of it, then that's the best you can do right now."

In Brian's room are pictures of the Blue Angels and Thunderbirds. On his desk, where he spends much of his afternoons e-mailing friends, is a baseball fouled off by Edgar Martinez, a former Seattle Mariner. Letters from John F. Kennedy and Robert Kennedy are framed and hanging on

Saved Twice

his wall. The letter from Robert Kennedy is dated September 28, 1964, and urges Brian to "keep up your marvelous courage and spirit."

The world record holder's mouth opened as the spoonful of soup neared. It's lunchtime. The arms that made him the world's first pole vaulter to attempt 17 feet are now lifeless and unable to help feed him.

The muscular body that arched over the bar that made him a world record holder sits motionless in a wheelchair. Yet like that young 19-year-old who soared to world record heights, Brian Sternberg still has the determination of an athlete.

As he often has, Brian talked not long ago to a group of athletes at a Fellowship of Christian Athletes camp. Speaking in almost a whisper, he said he never wanted any of them to face what he has faced. He never wanted them to be confined to a wheelchair, dependent on someone else to meet their every need.

"Unless," he said, "that's what it takes for you to put God in the center of your life."

Chapter 4

Don't Cut It Off

§&

All it took was Glen Dykstra's quiet nod of approval.
And his two-year-old son's bloodied right arm, mangled in a grain auger that morning on the family's farm, would be gone. Amputated at the shoulder.

But Glen, a high school basketball legend in this small farm town in northwest Washington, wanted to wait. Just to make sure.

"He'll never have use of that arm," the doctor said quietly.

Glen, his eyes brimming with tears, firmly shook his head no.

"Let's just see how he heals," he said.

So amputation waited. A reprieve for a month.

And little Grant Dykstra's torn right arm, broken in three places and needing 260 stitches to close, did heal. Better than anyone hoped. Tearful prayers were answered. Doctors called it a miracle. But Grant, the youngest of three children, sees it more as a blessing. Whoever heard of a one-armed basketball player?

"I'm just thankful they didn't amputate," Grant said. "I'd never be able to play basketball."

Saved Twice

Twenty years and thirteen arm surgeries later, Grant was a basketball wonder, an all-conference, 6'4" guard for Western Washington University despite not having full use of a right arm that is five inches shorter than his left. Growth of his right arm was impeded by yearly surgeries from when he was five to twelve, the last coming the summer after sixth grade. Today he still can't close his right hand into a fist. He still can't move his right index finger without moving his middle finger because both fingers were surgically attached to the same tendon. And he still can't lift as much with his right arm as with his left.

The differences were obvious to an opposing coach.

"All the time I hear coaches yelling, 'Make him go right,'" Grant said.

And a defender would get up into Grant's left hand, leaving him no option but to go right. He obliged, dribbled right, quickly cut back left after shaking a defender and pulling up for a wide-open, left-handed jump shot. Swish. The coach's instructions were bad advice. Again.

"He's a courageous kid," said Brad Jackson, Grant's coach at Western Washington. "He's probably always had people say he couldn't do it. But he was always the best kid on the team he played on growing up."

Grant's is a remarkable story of overcoming, of encouraging parents who ignored desires to protect, of a young boy who never questioned God and merely accepted his fate. He had a lot of reasons not to play basketball. But even as a first grader, with his arm in a cast after yet another surgery, he'd go to a summer basketball camp, dribbling and shooting with his left hand even though he was naturally right-handed.

"I never thought about quitting. All my friends played basketball. My brother and sister played basketball. I just wanted to be like them."

But he was never like them. He was always better, starting on his high school varsity team as a freshman. He

28

Saved Twice

was named the state's 2A player of the year his senior year. Just as his dad, brother and sister did before him in Everson, Washington, Grant would be a starter at Lynden Christian and lead his team to a state title. As a four-year starter he broke school records for points, 3-pointers, assists, steals and free-throw percentage.

"Grant is about as competitive as any kid I've coached," Jackson said. "I don't think he's got anything to prove. He just loves to compete."

Refusing to let a handicap become an excuse, Grant was presented the Most Courageous Award for 2005 by the NCAA, a national honor given by the U.S. Basketball Writers' Association. He led Western Washington, a nationally ranked NCAA Division II team his junior year in scoring (17.4), was third in rebounding (5.3) and shot 51 percent from the field and 49.3 percent from 3-pointers.

"Doctors still tell me they're amazed," Grant said. "They say I'm a miracle."

He is also a survivor, finding strength in a supportive family and in his unbending faith in Jesus.

"Growing up, my parents would never allow us to say can't," Grant said. "Sometimes I would think, 'I can't.' But they'd always remind me that through Christ you can do all things."

The accident that changed Grant's life occurred early one May afternoon in 1984 when his cousins were playing at the Dykstras' 300-acre dairy farm that's three miles from the Canadian border. Two days after his second birthday he was playing hide-and-seek in the barn. Somehow his jacket sleeve got caught in the grain auger, which crushes and dispenses feed to the cows. The rotating machinery pulled his red coat in, clamping down on his arm. Unable to pull free, he screamed for help.

"One of my cousins ran downstairs to the milking parlor where my mom was working," Grant said.

Saved Twice

Frantically, the cousin told Alice Dykstra her son was hurt and needed help. Alice ran for the hayloft. Then she stopped.

"She said the presence of God came on her and turned her around to turn the machinery off," Grant said. "She didn't know yet that I was caught in the auger."

Alice's decision saved her son's life. By the time Alice reached the switch, the auger had Grant up to his shoulder.

"My head was going in next," he said.

Gently, Alice tried to pull him free but couldn't. It took Grant's dad and grandfather ninety minutes to take the auger apart so the paramedics could rush him to the hospital. Paramedics had suggested amputating.

Grant's red jacket, wrapped tightly around his arm, acted like a tourniquet.

"Otherwise I would have bled to death," he said.

After a month in the hospital he went home, with a right arm.

For several months his arm remained sewn to his stomach to help with the grafting. Beginning at age three he underwent yearly corrective surgeries, followed by physical therapy. Most of his surgeries were scheduled for the summers so he wouldn't miss school.

Basketball was his best physical therapy. His Christian faith was his best motivation.

"As a kid I heard the Bible stories in our family devotions," Grant said. "I'd hear stories about how God did things for a reason. I'd think or ask, why did this happen to me? My folks would explain that God has a plan for me. Now I can see this is why it happened."

Because of his inspiring story Grant, with his accomplishments and awards on the basketball court, has received national publicity. His story has been in USA Today and on ESPN. He was a finalist his senior year for the V Foundation

Saved Twice

Comeback Award for the second straight year. He has always shared his Christian faith.

"I have an opportunity to go and tell people about Jesus," Grant said. "What could be better?"

It's not a coincidence basketball has become his podium. He comes from a basketball family. His dad was nicknamed "The Legend," earning all-state honors at the same high school Grant attended and leading them to a 1976 state title. Grant's sister, Shannon, was a three-time all-state guard for Lynden Christian. His brother, Greg, was all-state in basketball and football and was an all-conference receiver at Western Washington University.

At age 14, Grant beat The Legend in H-O-R-S-E for the first time. That same year he played on his dad's church team when not enough adult players showed.

"I was the little kid popping threes. I'll always remember that day," Grant said.

Besides his 13 surgeries on his arm, he had two on the ankle he broke playing football in seventh grade and one on his knee to repair a torn anterior cruciate ligament injured while playing basketball as a sophomore. But surgeries never slowed him down.

"All the surgeries and all the physical therapy gave me more of an appreciation for basketball," he said.

The ease with which he plays the game hides a young life filled with surgeries and struggles and a basketball career that nearly ended before it started, saved by his dad's refusal to amputate.

"Basketball was something we were always doing," he said. "It made me feel more accepted."

To sit on the sidelines, watching, was to be different, to be an outsider. Playing basketball was a way of fitting in.

He now plays for Ws—winning and witnessing.

31

Saved Twice

"When I'm on the court I feel I am a representative of God," he said. "I try to show that." Grant turned a hardship into an opportunity.

"God has given us all an ability to do something," he said. "That's how you can showcase your love for Christ. Tell other people about Christ through that talent. God has given me the ability to play basketball."

Chapter 5

Running Scared

§§

Their smiles belie a horrid past. Their joyous eyes, so white against the blackest of skin, like the moon in a midnight sky, contradict their journey with death.

They've traveled an unimaginable distance to come here, past the giraffes and hippos of their native village in southern Sudan, past the unmarked graves on the fringe of their refugee camp in northern Kenya.

They've fled barefoot through jungles as far as 1,200 miles, a distance stretching from Seattle to Los Angeles. They've been chased on horseback by Sudanese soldiers, stalked by lions hidden in the tall Savanna grass, hunted by crocodile while swimming the Gilo River to reach Ethiopia.

They've been called The Walking Skeletons and The Lost Boys of Sudan.

They've endured an arduous journey, orphans of a 19-year war that has killed two million and forced another five million to flee their homes. One in seven Sudanese has been displaced in the bloodiest war since World War II.

"What is so astonishing is there is such a sweetness about them," said Betsy Higley, program manager for the Catholic Community Services in Washington that helped 30 Lost Boys resettle in the Tacoma area. "After all the horror they've been through, there's a joy there. That's Jesus. That's the fruit of their faith."

The war in Sudan is between north and south forces; light and dark skin; Muslims and Christians. Looting, massacres and enslavement are its strategies. Villages have been wiped out by frequent air raids, flattening hospitals, schools and churches.

The war reached Gabriel Atem's village in southern Sudan in 1989, six years after the civil war resumed. The First Civil War began in 1955, with the arrival of independence from the British, and ended in 1972.

"I was playing with a friend outside my hut when I heard guns fire," said Gabriel, who is from the Dinka tribe and was raised in a Christian home. "Everyone began running."

More machine guns fired. Smoke rose from the other side of his village as raiding soldiers torched huts.

"I didn't have time to look for my parents," Gabriel said. "I just ran."

He never saw his parents again.

Gabriel and hundreds of other boys ran into a field of Savanna grass so high and thick it hid them. While only five years old, he ran for an hour. He stopped after two hours when his legs became too tired to go on. Another boy, a teenager, told Gabriel to climb onto his back. He carried him well into the night.

Finally they lay in the tall Savanna grass, catching a fitful sleep. Huddled together under the starry African sky, they listened, afraid the soldiers would capture them.

"We knew we couldn't go back," Gabriel said. "We knew we couldn't stop or we'd die."

He knew of people who had refused to renounce their faith in Jesus Christ and were shot by the raiding Sudanese army. Many of the Lost Boys are Christians.

As days turned into weeks, more boys fleeing the Sudanese troops joined them, until hundreds of them were

Saved Twice

moving to Ethiopia where they could be safe. They didn't know 20,000 boys from throughout southern Sudan were doing the same thing.

With no food Gabriel ate a handful of yellow clay, or bark peeled from a Pach tree, or clumps of grass and leaves. Walking in temperatures exceeding one hundred degrees, he was told to drink his own urine to keep from dehydrating. And if a boy had no urine, another boy, fashioning a cup from clay, passed him his. On rare occasions when one of the boys killed an antelope with a spear, they'd squeeze the animal's stomach to get something to drink before eating the animal.

"There was not much to eat or drink," Gabriel said. "You did what you could to live. Many starved."

One morning, as they walked through the jungle, a lion pounced from the tall Savanna grass, snatching a boy not far from Gabriel, dragging the screaming boy back into the grass. Everyone ran.

Three months after Gabriel fled the soldiers who had invaded his village he reached the banks of the Gilo River, which separates Sudan and Ethiopia. Thousands of Lost Boys had camped along the river. Several days later they heard the fire of machine guns in the distance. They heard the roar of trucks coming closer. The Sudanese army was approaching. The boys' dilemma was whether to face the bullets or the crocodiles. Quickly hundreds of boys waded into the Gilo, some swimming and others floating as they clung to mats made of grass.

Boys, snatched by crocodiles or unable to swim, disappeared all around Gabriel. The water turned to a bloody river. Many didn't reach Ethiopia. Those who did wearily walked into a refugee camp, where they lived for the next three years in mud huts. In relative safety, Gabriel lay down each night on a grass bed, sleeping about ten in a hut the size of a small garage. The crowded darkness, smell of smoke

35

Saved Twice

and sweat and rasping coughs made it difficult to sleep. Many of those who coughed didn't survive. An older boy who became Gabriel's friend guarded him from the draft of the open doorway each night with his own body. Without this older boy Gabriel would have had no one.

"The elders would help. Without the elders I would not have survived. I know this," Gabriel said. "You just prayed for protection."

At the edge of camp stood a cemetery of unmarked graves. Familiar faces sometimes wouldn't appear in the lines for food, and everyone knew where they were. Their fight was over.

"I didn't know what would happen tomorrow," Gabriel said. "It is God who knows what will happen in the future. My condition was difficult, but I just handed myself to God and asked Him to take me in His hands."

After three years Gabriel and about 20,000 other Lost Boys had to run again as war broke out in Ethiopia. Again fleeing for his life as Sudanese government planes bombed the rear of their procession, he walked about 600 miles to Kenya where he found safety at the Kakuma refugee camp. An extension of grass huts and corrugated metal that stretched in a nearly continuous roofline for 10 miles became home for 70,000 people.

The camp, supported largely by the United Nations and church relief groups, became Gabriel's home for eight years. In makeshift schools, with dirt and sticks for paper and pencils, he learned to read and speak English. Then one day his teacher said, "Some of you will be able to go to the United States."

Stunned silence followed.

"We were all so excited," Gabriel said. "We had read about the United States. We knew what this meant."

36

Saved Twice

Boys crowded around a bulletin with a list of names nailed to a tree, and Gabriel saw his name. He was going to the U.S.

"I was so happy I cried," he said.

In December 2000, when Gabriel climbed into an airplane for the first time to leave Kenya and later landed in Seattle, a new life awaited him and he walked into a new world. He had never flipped on a light switch, never seen a television, never used a telephone, never ridden in a car, never seen a can opener or a fork. Someone said to him one day: "This is pizza."

Gabriel, along with 12 other boys dressed in similar white T-shirts and blue sweatpants, walked from the plane and into a new world. They had arrived without money or coats or luggage. A lady waiting for them there gave one shivering boy her coat. A few carried Bibles. They all brought papers from their school in Kakuma that they had carefully stuck in a small knapsack.

"It was all so strange," Gabriel said. "We had come to America. Wow. This was wonderful."

That night Gabriel slept in a room by himself for the first time in his life.

"They were happy and scared," said Mary McCarthy, who, along with her husband, became foster parents for Gabriel and two other Lost Boys. "Gabriel had nightmares when he first came. But not anymore."

Many of the boys who have come to Seattle share the same birth date, January 1. It's the date given to displaced people who have no birth records and don't know their birthdates.

About 100 Lost Boys resettled in the Seattle area that stretches from Everett to Centralia, a hundred-mile span. Sixty of them were under 18 and were placed in high schools.

Saved Twice

"Almost all of them feel they were chosen by God," Betsy Higley said. "They feel special because they made it. They feel they are here because of God, and they are very respectful of that. They go to church every Sunday, read their Bibles. They draw a lot of strength from their faith."

They have adapted to a modern world. In high school, Gabriel ran on the school's cross-country and track teams, worked at a grocery store and earned mostly Bs on his report card. He became a talented runner, reaching state in track and cross-country his junior and senior years. He once ran for his life, fleeing the Sudanese army. Then he ran for fun.

"I love running," Gabriel said. "Running is fun. I like pushing myself."

Betsy Higley said none of the Lost Boys has gotten into trouble with the law or with schools.

"Since they grew up without parents and families, it's hard to understand where they got this moral code," Higley said. "But they have it."

Gabriel doesn't have pictures of his parents. He has only memories, and those are fading. He doesn't know if his father, Abraham, and his mother, Amour, are alive. His village no longer exists. His people are scattered.

"It's not safe to go back," he said. "I won't go back to Sudan as long as there is war."

Now, for the first time since he was little, he has a family. He calls his foster parents Mom and Dad. This is his home. He is no longer afraid. He is not only at peace with God, but with his neighbor.

For 12 years he wandered. He is one of the Lost Boys. But he no longer feels lost. He is no longer an orphan of a war.

"I am glad to be here," Gabriel said. "They call us the Lost Boys. But we are not lost. We are found here in America. Here it is safe. There is no war here."

Chapter 6

Surviving An Avalanche

§§

Her team of climbers stretched below her, their brightly colored packs of red, blue and yellow in sharp contrast to the snow. At 11,600 feet, they slowly hiked down the steep face of Mount Rainier, five climbers connected by 150 feet of nylon rope.

As the guide, Ruth Mahre was the last one on the rope, ready to self-arrest if someone slipped on the 40-degree slope. Their five-day outing was coming to an end.

Four hours earlier, at 10 a.m., they reached the summit of the 14,410-foot peak, spending an hour at the top of the third-tallest mountain in the United States before beginning their long descent.

It was a gorgeous day. The air was still, and a blue sky with an occasional puffy cloud stretched below them. They could see snow-capped peaks along the jagged Cascade Range that reached into Oregon.

Because of unusually warm weather, they stuffed their down parkas into their packs and wore only shirt-sleeves. With the temperature in the high 50s, the snow was

Saved Twice

slushy, resulting in unstable footing even though they wore crampons.

"Slow your pace, Scott," Mahre yelled through cupped hands.

Scott Pressman, a 47-year-old ophthalmologist from Idaho, looked back over his shoulder and raised his ice ax to acknowledge Mahre's instructions. Other than Mahre, Pressman was the most experienced climber of the group. That's why Mahre put him at the lead. The others – Allen Fedor, Patrick Nestler and Nina Redman – were making their first big climb. The members of the group had come from Connecticut, Minnesota, Idaho and California, spending $745 each for the training and climbing expedition.

A month earlier, in May, Mahre had completed his master's degree in physical therapy, and she was working as a guide for the summer. It was only her third week on the job and second climb as a guide, but she was no novice to climbing Rainier. Her father, an avid climber, made sure his family knew all about climbing. That included her twin brothers, Steve and Phil, who medaled in the 1984 Winter Olympics in downhill skiing.

Being the younger sister of two Olympic skiers had its advantages. But sometimes she felt she was always trying to measure up to being a Mahre.

At this point of the climb, all she was thinking about was getting her team safely off the mountain.

Their ascent began at 3 o'clock that morning from Camp Muir at 10,000 feet, and they reached the summit by 10 a.m. Now at 2 p.m., Mahre knew everyone's legs were tired as they hiked parallel to Disappointment Cleaver, a long outcrop of volcanic rock, on the steepest section of the climb. It was a risky area because of the potential for rockslides.

At the base of the cleaver was a fixed rope that stretched nearly 300 feet, anchored by three steel rods. A climbing

Saved Twice

party just ahead of them had already clipped into the safety line.

"Go ahead and clip into the rope," Mahre yelled to Pressman.

He attached his carabineer to the waist-high safety rope. It was an act that nearly cost Mahre her life.

Minutes after Pressman clicked into the fixed line, someone in a climbing party behind Mahre yelled, "Slide!"

Above Mahre to her right, she spotted a basketball-sized snowball. Then a small slab of snow gave way. It headed directly toward the rope team below Mahre's group.

"Slide!" she yelled.

Four heads immediately looked up. The slide quickly gained in mass, growing to 30 yards wide and 10 feet deep.

"Run!" Mahre yelled.

It was too late. Wearing full packs and crampons and being clipped to a rope, they couldn't outrun the slide that was moving 25 miles an hour and gaining speed. A wave of snow buried the climbers ahead of Mahre's group, knocking them off their feet and sweeping them toward a cliff.

"Self-arrest!" Mahre screamed.

Falling to her stomach, she frantically dug her ice ax and the tips of her crampons into the snow. Redman and Nestler also tried to self-arrest.

It didn't help.

Because of the slushy snow, Mahre couldn't get a solid bite. The avalanche ripped the aluminum anchors out of the permanent safety line that both climbing teams were clipped into. Since they were hooked into the safety line, the avalanche pulled Mahre's group of climbers too, tossing them like rag dolls down the mountain.

There was a thunderous roar.

Mahre again jabbed her ice ax into the snow in hopes of stopping her group. But each time, she was flipped to her back, yanked by the rope. She tumbled over and over. Her

Saved Twice

world became a blur of snow and blue sky. Then Mahre saw a brown stretch of rocks and braced for the impact. Instead, she went airborne, launched over the rocks on a wave of snow and fell nearly 20 feet. She lost her ice ax in midair.

Mahre was certain she was going to die.

"Please God, save us," she prayed.

Suddenly, everything stopped. Mahre smashed into a huge bolder. The rope in her harness yanked tight as the weight of the other climbers pulled violently against her. Miraculously, their fall stopped. Relief overwhelmed Mahre. Wedged, she dangled, unable to touch the ground as the rope pulled her tight against the rock.

For several seconds, the avalanche poured over the climbers. Mahre pressed her face into the rock, praying. Finally, the avalanche stopped. There was silence. Then cries for help.

Afraid someone would unclip from the rope, Mahre yelled, "Nobody move! Any movement, and we're all going down!"

The nylon rope – their lifeline – was badly frayed, and the climbers hung by only a few strands. A second rope, the fixed line Scott had hooked into, also was on the verge of snapping.

Right below Mahre, Redman screamed hysterically.

"Help is coming," Mahre said. "Just try to remain calm."

Afraid to move, Mahre lay on her left side and couldn't see anyone below her. She spotted Pressman, who had landed on a rock parallel to Mahre about 70 feet away. The remaining seven climbers hung below Mahre in the shape of an upside-down horseshoe. Several were dangling, with a long drop into a crevasse below them.

The avalanche had dragged them about 350 feet.

"Everyone just stay still!" Mahre yelled. "A rescue team will get here soon!"

Saved Twice

Mahre's left hip ached, but she had no gashes or broken bones. Carefully, she brushed the snow from her face.

About 100 feet below Mahre, Nestler dangled over the face of a rock, the spray of melting snow soaking his clothes. He was vulnerable and needed medical attention, but rescuers couldn't get to him. Occasionally, Mahre heard him yell for help.

After only a few minutes, Mahre spotted Tyler Forman, a fellow guide and her older sister's son, running across the snow to reach them. He had been leading a climbing party behind them.

"Stop running!" Mahre yelled. "That whole hillside could come down on us!"

Tyler stopped in his tracks.

"Help is on the way!" he yelled.

Before long, three guides peeked over the cliff. They radioed for help and a helicopter. A climber below Mahre, Deborah Lynn from California, dangled underneath a small waterfall from melting snow and was the first priority. With no jacket on, she was in danger of hypothermia.

"I'm OK!" Mahre yelled. "Get to Debbie first!"

But before they went after anyone, guides took the ropes from three other climbing parties, found a safe place for them and anchored Mahre's line.

Two guides then rappelled down to Lynn, who had slipped into shock. When they unclipped her from the rope, Mahre dropped several inches, scaring her.

Lynn collapsed. A guide tried unsuccessfully to piggy-back her up the cliff and ended up putting her in a parka and going to help others.

Twenty-nine-year-old Nestler, soaked and shivering, was slipping in and out of consciousness by the time rescuers reached him about 7:30 p.m. An attempt to reach him earlier failed because the rescue group didn't have enough rope.

43

Saved Twice

Mahre lay as still as she could for five hours before a guide rappelled down to her and helped her out of the rope and onto a ledge. She then prusiked to safety. Mahre hadn't been able to move or unclip from the rope because everyone else would have slid down the mountain.

"Thank God, we're safe," Mahre said, cheerfully hugging people after getting off the cliff.

By 7:45 p.m., all of the climbers were safely off the face of the cliff and on their way to a hospital in a helicopter. Injuries included several broken legs and hands, hypothermia and shock. Mahre had a bruised back and bruised left thigh.

She stayed behind, helping a climbing party that had been waiting behind them. She reached Camp Muir at 10 p.m. It wasn't until then that Mahre heard about the death of Nestler, the climber from Connecticut, who had died from exposure. She was stunned.

But five days later, Mahre guided another team up Mount Rainier and made 30 climbs to the summit that summer.

Her accident taught her something about humility and about her relationship with God, the Creator.

"I have a new reverence when I'm in God's presence during prayer," Mahre said. "Sometimes we think we're pretty important. Sometimes we forget who God is, and we get a little too buddy-buddy, a little too familiar. There is no better way to appreciate God than to be in His creation, and maybe nothing better than the mountains to feel just how minuscule we are."

Humility is a prerequisite in a relationship with God.

"Because of an avalanche, I understand that," Mahre said. "And I accept it."

Chapter 7

Dead on Arrival
§§

Kayla Burt sat on the edge of her bed, listening to the eleven o'clock news.

"Loree," she said. "I'm not so sure I'm going to stay awake until midnight."

It was New Year's Eve, thirty minutes away from the moment people around the world celebrate. Six of Kayla's teammates from the University of Washington's basketball had come over to her rented house in Seattle for a low-key party. They spent the evening munching pizza, watching a forgettable rented movie (Trap, with Kevin Bacon) and downing pop and chips.

The next morning they had practice at eight o'clock.

"Come on, Kaaaayla. Don't be such a baby," said Loree Payne, Kayla's best friend and teammate. "It's New Year's Eve."

Kayla began feeling dizzy.

"Loree, I'm feeling kind of lightheaded," she said, rubbing her forehead.

Suddenly she collapsed and fell face first onto the floor.

"That's really funny, Kayla," Loree said as she looked at her friend lying on the floor. "Really funny. Get up."

She didn't move.

Saved Twice

"Kayla?"

Still no movement.

Loree turned Kayla over and saw that she was unconscious and wasn't breathing. She was turning blue.

"Kayla!" Loree screamed. "Somebody, quick! Help! Kayla's not breathing. Oh, dear God, help us!"

Loree grabbed the phone and dialed 911. Giuliana and Gioconda Mendiola, twin sisters who had been downstairs, rushed into the room. Erica Schelly, a freshman guard, wasn't far behind.

"Here, Erica! Quick! Take the phone," Loree shouted then ran from the room to get help from a neighbor.

Quickly the sisters lifted Kayla onto the bed.

"She's turning purple!" Gio shouted. "We've got to get her some air."

Kayla was dying. Her heart had stopped, and she wasn't breathing. Gio, remembering what she'd seen on a TV cop show, began blowing puffs of air into her mouth, filling her lungs. Giuliana began pushing on Kayla's chest, hoping to get her heart started.

"You guys. I don't know what I'm doing," Gio said in desperation. "I've only seen this on TV."

Erica had remained on the phone with the 911 dispatcher. Calmly the dispatcher began giving Erica instructions. Erica relayed the instructions on how to properly do CPR.

"Pull her head back to open her throat up," she said. "Hold her nose."

Gio pinched Kayla's nose.

"Breath into her," Erica said. "Fifteen compressions to the chest. Then two breaths."

Kayla's chest rose as Gio's breath filled her lungs with air, bringing oxygen to her brain and preventing long-term damage.

Saved Twice

Within several minutes sirens could be heard. Paramedics, carrying a gurney, rushed into the room, taking over the rescue. They pulled out the electrical shockers.

"Clear," the paramedic said before jolting Kayla.

The flat line on the monitor skipped; then a regular heartbeat resumed. The machine began to beep.

"Her heart is beating on its own," a relieved paramedic said. "Let's get her to the hospital."

Kayla went from death to life. This was how fast life could be taken. Later that night a doctor, with Kayla's parents standing by their daughter's bedside as she lay unconscious, told them she had a rare and incurable genetic disorder called Long QT Syndrome. It had caused irregularities in her heartbeat, resulting in its stopping.

"We're going to have to put in a defibrillator," the doctor said.

With tears rolling down her cheeks, Kayla's mother, Teri, squeezed her daughter's hand as she lay in a coma.

Three days later, after regaining consciousness, Kayla underwent surgery. A one-and-a-half-inch by one-and-a-half-inch box was implanted on the right side of her chest. It would be a constant companion and a permanent safeguard, monitoring her heartbeat and applying shocks to correct irregularities.

"You'll never be able to play basketball again," the doctor told Kayla after surgery. "You can lead a normal life. But you'll never be able to play basketball competitively again."

Just like that, basketball was gone. The game that had meant so much to Kayla was taken because of a genetic heart ailment passed on by her great-grandfather. The game she had played since third grade, the game in which she had been a high school all-American, was gone.

"Never?" Kayla repeated.

The doctor shook his head no.

Saved Twice

The sophomore guard was leading the Pac-10 in three-point shooting percentage, averaging eight points, and was on a team headed for the NCAA playoffs.

Basketball had been such an important part of her life.

"I've lost the game, but I haven't lost my friends," Kayla said. "I haven't lost my life."

Through this hardship she discovered something about herself and about the power of a testimony. To her surprise she became an inspiration and a witness to her teammates, classmates and coaches.

Kayla's brush with death changed the focus of her life from being the girl who could shoot three-pointers to the one who cheated death. And to the one who talked about God. People listened.

Right after the surgery Loree visited Kayla in the hospital, bringing flowers and a get-well card. Carefully Loree leaned down to hug her best friend.

"Well, Kayla," Loree said. "When are you getting out of this place?"

Kayla smiled back.

"I'm getting out of here soon," she said. "You know, it's a miracle I'm alive. I'm thankful to God for that. It wasn't a coincidence you were there when I collapsed. If that had happened when I was sleeping I wouldn't be here."

That continued to be Kayla's message. She shared her gratitude for her teammate's quick actions. And she talked about her appreciation and acknowledgment of a loving and caring God.

A couple of days after Kayla was released from the hospital she stood on the sideline with her teammates moments before a home game against Arizona State. Her teammates were in uniform, wearing purple and white. Kayla was in street clothes.

"It felt strange. It was game time, and I wasn't going to play," Kayla said.

Saved Twice

The gym was packed. Before he named the starting lineups, the announcer roared, "Here's Kaaaayla Buuuuurt!"

She walked to middle court and waved to the crowd. Fans stood and cheered. The gym shook. It was an incredible moment.

After basketball practice a week following Kayla's surgery, Sunny Smallwood, one of Washington's assistant coaches, put an arm around her.

"You know, you've really helped me," Sunny said.

Kayla wondered what she had done. She hadn't realized that simply by sharing her faith and trust in Jesus she had encouraged Sunny.

"You've really helped my faith," Sunny said. "I've been slipping away from God because I've been more worried about basketball. But I've watched you and your testimony, and you've helped me get things turned around."

Kayla was surprised and pleased by her coach's comments.

"That's God working through me," Kayla said. "He can do the same thing through you."

Her dramatic New Year's Eve had somehow made people more transparent, more open. Death, the unspoken endpoint for us all, was a headline story. It made people vulnerable to her message of hope in Jesus.

"It's really not about me," Kayla said. "It's about God. He's been my strength in all this. In my weakness He's strong. I've cried, but I've been so happy. Happy to be around people. I know that's Him. That's not me. That's Him working through me."

Two years earlier, Kayla met Loree for the first time. Kayla had just become a Christian her senior year in high school. It was Loree who helped Kayla's faith grow by encouraging her to read the Bible and pray. That foundation helped Kayla share her Christian faith after her encounter with death.

Saved Twice

At school, classmates Kayla had never met kept telling her she was such an inspiration. People were so friendly.

"I saw you on TV," they'd say. "You're something else."

For the next couple of weeks, Kayla's mailbox was packed with cards and gifts. All the local daily newspapers and television stations did stories about Kayla, so what she had been through wasn't a secret.

"You mean so much to me," one person wrote. "I'm so encouraged by your life."

For the rest of the season Kayla went to every practice. Once the incision for her defibrillator healed she started shooting baskets again. She beat the team manager in a game of H-O-R-S-E. And she sometimes went through lay-up drills with the team. But she didn't do anything too strenuous.

So life goes on. Without basketball. A little zapper in Kayla's chest won't let her heart stop again. She's safe. That's good. But life is different and will never be the same again. That's hard.

"There is no way I could have endured this by myself. I've leaned on God through this whole thing," Kayla said. "His strength is what's kept me going."

Chapter 8

A Miraculous Comeback

Ⴛ&

In a gray, early morning light, Shelley Harder walked alone across the bridge to move orange road construction cones as traffic drove by.

It was about 4:30 a.m., nearing the end of her work shift as a flagger on a stretch of Interstate-5 through Bellingham, Wash. The temporary lighting had been shut off and a crew that looked like silhouettes to oncoming traffic worked on the shoulder.

Traffic slowed as it funneled from two lanes to one.

A green pickup suddenly skidded and slammed into an orange traffic barrel, sending it skidding down the shoulder of the road. Everyone on the work crew heard the screech. Judging from the skid marks, the pickup truck was traveling 55 mph.

Brian West, a state inspector at the job site, went over and talked with the driver.

"Are you all right?" West asked.

"Yeah, I'm fine," driver said.

Then he drove off.

But no one knew Shelley, an all-state guard her senior year in high school, had been hit by that skidding barrel.

51

Saved Twice

The sound of the screeching tires scared all the workers and they decided to take a head count. They quickly realized Shelley was missing. Someone said Shelley had gone to a portapotty a couple of exists down. Someone else said they had driven her back.

Shelley was supposed to be with them.

A search began. After a few minutes, a worker found Shelley's two-way radio on the bridge over Squalicum Creek.

"Someone put two-and-two together really fast and they looked over the side of the bridge deck with some flash lights," said Tim Harder, Shelley's dad.

Someone spotted Shelley, lying motionless on her back in some bushes.

"There she is," they yelled. "Quick down here. Hurry."

The rush to save Shelley's life began.

The orange 25-pound traffic barrel slid about 70 feet, slamming into Shelley and knocking her backwards from the bridge. The impact of the barrel tore a chunk from her arm and fractured her pelvis. A 35-foot fall broke her shoulder, back, ribs and wrist, lacerated her liver, spleen and kidney, and caused severe bleeding in her brain.

It was amazing she was alive.

Harder grew up playing sports and fell in love with basketball. She'd shoot baskets for hours in her family's driveway in the small farm town of Everson, Wash. She was a first-team all-conference selection two years at Nooksack Valley High School. After redshirting her freshman year at Saint Martin's University, Shelley's coach, Tim Healy, called her the best shooter on the team and she was expected to play an important role.

But the accident that nearly took her life robbed her of that chance to play. She'd never play basketball again.

Saved Twice

About 15 minutes after the accident, Shelley was found. Conscious when rescuers reached her, Shelley gave them her parent's home phone number.

At 5:20 a.m., Tim, who was just about to head for work for the same road construction company Shelley was working for, answered the phone at his home.

"They told us to come to the jobsite because Shelley had been in an accident," Tim said. "I didn't think she was hurt bad because if she had been she would have been taken to the hospital."

Leaving a note for their 15-year-old son, Corey, Tim and his wife, Nancy, quickly headed for the accident.

"I didn't take my car because I thought I'd just drive Shelley home in her car," Nancy said.

However, on their way there, they got another phone call, telling them to go directly to the hospital in Bellingham.

"Then we started to think it was serious," Nancy said.

Shelley injuries were so bad she needed 30 units of blood in two days at the hospital.

By 2 o'clock in the afternoon, eight hours after the accident, 50 of Shelley's family and friends were in the hospital's waiting room, praying and anxiously hoping for a good report. About then, two doctors gave Tim and Nancy frightening news.

"They told us they didn't expect Shelley to live," Tim said. "Her brain injury was substantial."

Tim and Nancy had to make a decision on whether to leave Shelley on life support or let her die. They told the doctors to do all they could to save their daughter's life.

It wasn't until that evening that the Harders saw their daughter.

"Nancy went to her right side, I went to her left," Tim said, pausing to compose himself as he remembered the emotional scene. "I told Shelley I loved her. She squeezed my hand. I began to thank the Lord for Shelley's life."

Saved Twice

Tim then dropped to his knees and began to praise God.

"It was a very emotion moment," Tim said.

In surgery early that afternoon, doctors removed a five-inch portion of Shelley's skull to drain and scrape a massive hematoma. Pressure on her brain was measured at 30. Normal is nine and anything over 40 there is considerable risk of brain damage. The next day, her brain pressure spiked to 50.

Shelley was quickly moved into the operating room for emergency surgery.

"After a little bit, I saw the doctors again," Tim said. "I could tell by the way they were walking they had good news."

No surgery was necessary.

"They said they were trying to determine why the pressure went back down, but they didn't have an answer," Tim said.

Tim did. He and his wife credit prayer.

"We heard that every church in Whatcom County had a prayer chain going," Nancy said. "People had been praying for Shelley from the moment she reached the hospital. I believe in prayer. I believe Shelley is alive because of prayer."

After two days at the Bellingham hospital, Shelley was airlifted by helicopter to Harborview Medical Center in Seattle, where her long recovery continued.

Because of an air tube down her throat and later because of a tracheotomy, Shelley was unable to talk for over a month. She'd mouth words to communicate.

"I can't read lips at all," Tim said. "Finally, one day I figured out what she was saying. She was hot. I was so excited I called Nancy."

Doctors at Harborview called Shelley their "miracle patient." They didn't expect her to live.

Saved Twice

"It is a miracle," said Tim Healy, the Saint Martin's coach who recruited Shelley. "She's been through so much."

On Oct. 8, two months after her accident, Shelley was moved to the rehabilitation wing at Harborview and began to learn how to walk again. First, she had to stand.

"I was so excited to walk," said Shelley, who remembers nothing of the accident.

Standing between parallel bars, Shelley shuffled, steadying herself by the bars.

"I tried to walk a lot, but I was so jerky," she said. "I was disappointed. I thought it would be easier."

Throughout her rehabilitation, Shelley called friends, giving them updates and accomplishments.

"She'd say, 'I took four steps today.' She'd be so excited," said Sheryl Staudacher, a teammate and close friend at Saint Martin's.

When Shelley started walking up stairs, she'd call friends with the news.

"Shelley is still driven," Staudacher said. "She's very competitive. Feisty."

An accident cost Shelley a bright season on her basketball team. Amazingly, it didn't cost her life.

"I'm determined to play again," she said in a whisper. "But I don't know. Things aren't going as quickly as I had hoped."

She knows, as coaches like to say, only one speed – all out.

On Nov. 21, just a few days before Thanksgiving, Shelley was released from the hospital and went home.

"I was so happy to get out of that hospital," Shelley said.

Her brush with death has changed her. She cherishes the simplest of things – sitting by her parents, talking with friends, taking a short walk. But all the changes aren't good.

"I'm more cautious," she said. "I don't like that."

Saved Twice

Throughout the ordeal, Healy stayed in close contact with the Harders, calling them or receiving daily emails. During a dramatic, heart-wrenching time, the Harders' Christian testimony spoke the loudest.

"Her parents are amazing people," Healy said. "They're inspirational. They've made it easy for all of us struggling with this to be around them and around Shelley because they've never felt sorry for themselves."

For months after the accident, Shelley continued to go to physical and occupational therapy and speech therapy several times a week. She took an on-line course from Whatcom Community College. Shelley later underwent surgery on her shoulder, wrist and throat, yet she remained positive.

"I've tried to take this all as a compliment," Shelley said. "God only gives the toughest things to the strongest people."

Shelley, who once raced gracefully up and down a basketball court, now walks with a limp. For a long time, the straight-A student couldn't write her name because her fractured wrist was fused together.

"It's been very frustrating," she said about her slow recovery. "Very hard. I just have to be patient."

Her triumphs have come slowly. She spent three weeks in intensive care. A 10-inch incision in her abdomen was left open because of bleeding and swollen organs for two weeks. It was nearly two months before she walked. Unable to eat for two months, Shelley lost 30 pounds, her weight dropping from 135 to 105 as she was fed intravenously.

It was three months before she was released from the hospital.

After getting released, Shelley needed surgery to replace two five-inch skull fragments on both sides of her head that had been removed and stored on ice to alleviate pressure on her brain. She wore a helmet for protection.

Saved Twice

"Her hair had grown back about two inches," Tim Harder said. "She wasn't looking forward to a shave head again with stables."

It's been a bittersweet journey for Shelley and her parents. Tim and Nancy have endured the heartache of nearly losing their daughter. They've seen the power of prayer and they've been embraced by a community. Their daughter's brush with death focused their faith.

"The outpouring of love from Lacey to Bellingham has been amazing," Tim said. "I can't say how blessed we've been."

A man, who had lost a son in a car accident and had heard about Shelley's accident, told Tim he had been praying for Shelley.

"We thank God for Shelley's life," Nancy said. "We thank Him for giving her back to us."

Chapter 9

A Heart For God

§§

Milo Vela felt like he was trying to stop a Mac truck. During basketball practice, a shot went up and Vela struggled to screen out Ben DeVoe, a 6-foot-11, 285-pound center. Their legs tangled and they fell. Ben landed on Milo's chest.

"You all right?" Ben asked, helping Milo up.

"Ah, yeah," Milo stammered, bending over as he felt a sharp pain in my chest. "Yeah, fine."

The slender, 6-foot-1 Milo then sprinted down court. No problem, he thought. It was Milo's senior year, his first on the varsity as a backup guard on his high school team in Olympia, Wash. There was no way a little discomfort was going to stop him.

But over the next couple of days, he felt an annoying pain in his chest. He passed it off as a pulled cartilage, or a strained muscle. However, his clammy hands and shortness of breathe were harder to ignore.

He felt as if he were a five-pack-a-day chain smoker. Short of breathe. Little endurance. And there was an ache in his chest.

"Push yourself, Milo," John Kiley, the Olympia basketball coach, barked a few days later at practice.

58

Saved Twice

Milo never loafed. Now, it was like he was running in sand. Every sprint down the court was like a marathon. Even a little walk through the mall made him sweat.

"Mom, I want to see a doctor," Milo said one morning before heading to school. "I've got this pain in my chest."

That afternoon, a doctor squeezed Milo into his day's busy schedule and took some chest x-rays. Not thinking anything really serious was wrong, Milo's mom, Quina, let him drive alone to the appointment. The doctor didn't find anything serious. Thinking Milo had some inflammation from a pulled muscle, the doctor simply told Milo to take some Ibuprofen and sent him on his way. But a couple of days later, that same doctor reached Milo by phone, telling the senior guard he wanted to see him fast. He had bad news.

"Don't do anything physical," the doctor said in a serious voice. "You've got an enlarged heart."

Milo about dropped the phone.

The next morning, the doctor slapped two X-rays of Milo's heart down on a light table, showing Milo and his mom the simple truth. One picture was taken a couple of months earlier when Milo partially separated his shoulder scrambling for a loose basketball at a summer practice. The difference was obvious. His heart had almost doubled in size. Milo's mom gasped.

"I thought the doctor had made some kind of mistake,' Quina said. "I just couldn't believe it."

The membrane around Milo's heart had filled with fluid, a result of his collision with Ben.

"This is serious," the doctor said. "Sports are out. I don't even want you to get excited."

Milo felt his heart racing as the doctor said that.

"Don't get excited?" Milo thought. "Yeah right."

Over the next two days, Milo underwent a barrage of tests, including an EKG. It was then that doctors made another startling discovery. They found that Milo also had

Saved Twice

a leaky heart valve. Instead of three valve platelets, he had two. It was a birth defect.

"Aortic regurgitation," the doctor said.

That's another way of saying Milo was finished as a basketball player. Possibly forever. Certainly for his senior year. He couldn't practice. Running was out. He wasn't even supposed to argue with his younger sister. He'd have to be on blood thinners for the rest of my life. Surgery was imminent.

Milo's dad, Emilio, went into a crisis mode. He began reading everything he could find on the Internet about aortic regurgitation. That's how Milo's dad deals with stress. A couple of times, Emilio went into his son's room late at night to do some research on the computer. Milo woke with a start.

"It's all right," Milo's dad whispered. "I'm just going to do some research."

The next day after school Milo went to practice to watch. His teammates circled him, patted him on the back and wished him well. It was like Milo was at his own funeral. Everyone was so somber. His coach later talked to the team about donating blood for Milo's operation.

Milo couldn't believe this was happening to him. He was crushed. Since his freshman year, he had looked forward to playing for Coach Kiley. Milo had gone to all the summer camps and worked hard to be on the varsity team. Now, it was all taken from him. He couldn't believe it. There was a good chance he could have surgery in the next couple of days.

In a very somber meeting with his family that night, Emilio went over what his son faced. Dad set down some rules.

"Milo," he said. "You're not to get stressed out."

Immediately, Milo began to stress out.

Saved Twice

And then they prayed. Afterwards, Milo's mom called their church, asking for prayer. Quina also called her sister, whose husband is a pastor. She then called Emilio's dad's family. They all began to pray. That Sunday, just five days after the news about Milo's faulty heart and after he had seen a doctor every day that week, he went forward to be prayed for at church. His whole family went forward with him. Pastor Dale Ulmquist talked with Milo about faith.

"If you're going to be healed, you need to believe," he told Milo. "God doesn't work through people who don't believe."

Milo believed. Dale prayed for Milo, put oil on his forehead and instantly Milo felt healed.

When they got to our car, Milo told his mom he wanted to play basketball again.

"I want to go to the doctor to get approval to play," Milo said. "I really want to play basketball tomorrow."

Milo's mom just looked at him.

"What are you talking about?" she said. "You're not going to play basketball. We've been talking about surgery."

"But mom, when Pastor prayed for me, I felt healed," Milo said. "I know I can play."

There was utter quiet.

"Well," Quina finally said. "You're going to need a doctor's approval first."

Later that afternoon, Quina, a teacher at their church's elementary school, called the father of one of her students in her kindergarten class who is a doctor. Philip Jones is a cardiologist. Looking for a favor, Milo's mom asked if he could examine Milo the next morning. He agreed to see Milo at 8:30 a.m. in his office.

"I slept like a baby that night," Milo said. "I knew I was all right."

That next morning, Milo was sitting in Dr. Jones' examination room, with his shirt off, ready to hear the good news.

Saved Twice

The doctor put the stethoscope to Milo's chest. The room was absolutely quiet. He moved the stethoscope around, stared intently at the floor as he listened to Milo's heartbeat. Finally, he stood upright and a smile broke across his face.

"There's nothing the matter with your heart," Dr. Jones said. "If there was any inflammation, it isn't there any more."

Milo let out a hoot.

"Can I play basketball tonight?" Milo asked.

"Not yet," the doctor said, laughing.

Milo still had to undergo a barrage of tests. And Dr. Jones arranged for Milo to take those tests that Friday in a Seattle hospital. Rather than wait another three or four weeks, Milo had four days.

"It was the longest four days of my life," Milo said. "I was still a spectator at basketball practices, except now I yelled. I couldn't wait to play. I even took stats at one of our games."

Finally, Friday came. Doctors took an echo image of Milo's heart. It showed that his heart was the normal size. All the inflammation was gone.

Then they put Milo through another stress test, monitoring his heart as he ran on a treadmill for 30 minutes. With sweat pouring from Milo, the doctor said, "Your heart looks great."

"The doctor said he was getting bored watching," Milo said. "The doctors said they've never seen a heart like mine heal so fast."

Only two weeks earlier, Milo was told he needed surgery. Now, he was a poster child for good health. The same doctor who told Vela he'd need surgery within a few weeks revised his prognosis, saying surgery wouldn't be needed until Milo was in his 70s.

Saved Twice

"I'm just doing this so your coach can breathe easy," the doctor said as he monitored the results of the treadmill test. "I know your heart is fine."

Four different doctors gave Milo the go ahead to play basket again. He rejoined the team the next day, a Saturday morning practice.

"Milo handed me the doctor's release, saying he's good to go," Coach Kiley said. "We made sure it was signed. It's miraculous. Here he was, about to have open heart surgery any day, and he's back playing basketball."

Kiley had talked with his team about donating blood for Milo's surgery. Now, Vela was back with the team, running up and down court at practice, ready to resume his role as a back-up guard.

"This has all been bittersweet," said Milo, who had been going to doctors nearly every day for three weeks. "I'm just thankful I'm well."

His teammates swarmed around Milo as he walked onto the court. He felt good to be back. Then as he went through lay-up drills, he noticed something spectacular. No pain. He only felt the excitement of being back on the team, running up and down the court.

"It was amazing," Milo said. "I was like the lame guy in the Bible. Healed."

"Shoot the ball," Kiley yelled from the sidelines.

Milo shot and swished his first shot.

"Everyone knew I was a walking miracle," Milo said. "God really does hear and answer our prayers."

Chapter 10

Eyes On The Goal

§§

Quickly, the trainer cleaned Mark McHugh's bloodied left eye, dabbing a deep gash along his eyebrow that needed 12 stitches to close.

There was blood on the floor, on Mark's jersey and on the trainer's towel.

Moments earlier, Mark, his lanky, 6-foot-7 frame reaching for a rebound, was jabbed in the eye as a defender swatted at the ball. With just 30 seconds left in the game and with Mark's all-star basketball team from southwest Washington leading a team from Colorado by 20 points, a win was assured.

And Mark, a three-sport letterman who began receiving college recruiting letters going into his junior year at Centralia High School, was having the game of his life, scoring 20 points and pulling down 14 rebounds.

"Can you see?" the trainer asked.

Mark strained to see.

"Is my eye open?" he asked.

It was.

Three exams by three eye specialists over the next two weeks reached the same conclusion. Mark was blind in his left eye. The blow severed his optic nerve.

Saved Twice

Surgery wouldn't return his sight.

"I couldn't believe it," Mark said. "Blind. Me? It happened so fast."

And what happened next is more unexpected than the fist that took the sight in one eye of a 16-year-old boy in love with a game, in love with life and in love with a challenge. Rather than withdraw, rather than pull away from friends and rather than drop football, basketball and baseball, Mark worked even harder.

He'd regain his starting forward spot on the basketball team, averaging eight points and helping his team return to the state playoffs. He'd pitch on the junior varsity team and he'd start at quarterback.

"I had a hard time letting him out of my sight for a month, but I'm better now," said Dawn McHugh, Mark's mother. "Mark has handled this much better than I have. I just think it's taken a lot of courage."

And faith.

Mark's Christian faith hasn't waned. He's not challenged God, angrily asking "Why?" Instead, he does as his favorite Bible character, Job, does – praise God, no matter what the circumstances.

"Mark has a very strong faith in and God and he sees all of this having a purpose," Dawn said. "He feels his loss of sight can be to God's glory."

A week after Mark McHugh came home from Los Angeles, he shot a basketball for the first time since his accident at a hoop in his driveway.

"It was weird," Mark said.

With one eye, his depth perception was radically changed. It was something he'd struggle with as his mind learned to adapt.

"Doctors told me that eventually my depth perception would come back," he said.

Saved Twice

To relieve the pressure from a buildup of blood in Mark's eye, he had surgery several weeks after the accident. The day after surgery, Mark's high school basketball coach, Ron Brown, came over to console and to challenge. Rather than pity, Mark got a pep talk.

"He said he thought I was good enough to play and it's not going to affect me as much as I think," Mark said. "I don't really know if he gave me an option. He said, 'You're playing.'"

Brown, a Christian who has coached at the same high school for 41 years in Centralia, Wash., understood the value of a challenge in Mark's life.

"I wasn't going to let him use the eye as an excuse," Brown said. "He's a ballplayer. Some people aren't as tall, some people are slower, and you're still on them to be better. This is just something he has to deal with. I'm the coach and I'm just trying to help him get better. That was my approach."

On the first day of practice, Brown lined his players up, had them close their left eye and then had them extend their left arm straight out to the side.

"Now move your arm in until you can see your hand," Brown said.

Most of the players' hands were almost in front of them before they stopped.

"That's the challenge Mark faces," Brown said.

The nightmares have stopped. Mark's focus is on tomorrow, not the past. He no longer dreams about the accident. He's not fixated on the moment of the accident, replaying in his mind what he might have done to prevent it. He hasn't even thought about the kid who caused the injury.

"I don't think that kid knew how serious it was," Mark said. "Nobody did."

Mark carries no bitterness toward the player who left him blind in one eye.

66

Saved Twice

"That's just Mark," said Isaac Moog, Mark's teammate and best friend. "He's never said anything about it. He's never said anything about that kid."

Moog, who is also a Christian, has seen Mark's faith in God grow through this experience.

"When this first happened, he was obviously devastated," Moog said. "Not too long after that he said that God was going to gave him an opportunity to give his testimony."

Mark said he's going to follow God not just because of blessings. He's going to believe, obey and worship God because of who He is – God. It's easy to praise God when all is right.

"I think about Job," Mark said. "He never cried out to God. My faith has always been there. I'd go to church. But when something tragic happens like this, you rely on your faith and who God is."

Mark's adjustment to playing basketball with one eye was up and down through his first season after the injury. He struggled at times and was frustrated at times. But he never gave up. His scoring average dropped from 13.4 points to 8.5 points, and his shooting percentages dropped slightly. Yet he scored 19, 3 and 20 points in a three-game span late in the season.

Mark has been an inspiration to his teammates and to his coaches.

"Sometimes we whine about a stubbed toe or when things aren't going our way," said John Kiley, Mark's coach on the summer team. "Toughen up. Mark says this is the hand he's been dealt. So, his attitude has been, 'bring it on.' He's ready to meet the challenge. I admire his courage."

Every shot, every rebound and every pass now takes courage. With one eye, Mark's depth perception and range of vision are dramatically changed. Yet Mark is turning a tragedy into a triumph.

Saved Twice

"Mark's story is about handling adversity," Kiley said. "His story is going to be told again and again and again. He doesn't blame God. But he leans on Him."

Mark has talked with teammates, friends and church groups about facing challenges. He's become a source of inspiration, not pity. Despite losing sight in his left eye, Mark earned a basketball scholarship to Western Washington University.

"Mark is an amazing kid," Kiley said. "Sometimes we whine about things not going our way."

Mark just keeps on going, relying on his Christian faith. He's discovered being a Christian doesn't bring immunity to hardships.

And this tall, slender high school athlete discovered he can lean on God, draw strength and comfort in the good and bad times.

Chapter 11

Running From Danger

The teenaged gangster pressed the barrel of a pistol against Lorenzo Romar's temple and snarled, "What if I pulled this trigger?"

Lorenzo, frightened for his life, shut his eyes and waited.

As Lorenzo reflects on a life that began in a gang-filled neighborhood in southern California and has reached the heights of NCAA basketball, first as a player and now as a coach, he can't help but wonder, "What if?"

What if the gun-waving gang member who wanted to recruit Lorenzo had pulled the trigger? What if as a junior college guard struggling with his grades Lorenzo had quit school?

Perhaps the most amazing thing about Lorenzo's unlikely journey is not what he's become – the Pacific-10 Conference men's basketball coach of the year in 2004, when his Washington Huskies shocked the West with a 29-6 record, a conference championship and a ride to the third round of the NCAA tournament.

It's what he has not become: a gangbanger with a rap sheet, or a college dropout pumping gas. Lorenzo's achievement isn't as much what he has done as it is what he's overcome.

Saved Twice

"What kept me out of the gangs were my parents," Lorenzo said. "It was my fear of them. And it was also my fear that if I got messed up into this gang stuff, my basketball career was out the window. My love for sports kept me out of the gangs."

When Lorenzo was 14, a gang member pulled a pistol from under his shirt, pushed the barrel of the gun against Lorenzo's temple and snarled, "What if I pulled this trigger?"

"I was scared," Lorenzo said.

That was life in Compton, Calif., home of the notorious Crips and Bloods gangs.

When Lorenzo was 15, he was playing touch football with his younger brother and two friends in the street in front of their Compton home. A gang member pedaled up on his bicycle and asked if the Lorenzo brothers were going to join his gang.

"I said, 'Sure,'" Lorenzo said. "I wasn't going to, but I said that just so he'd go away. But my brother said, 'No. I'm not joining.'"

The gang member reached into a basket on his bike and pulled out a handgun from under a sweatshirt and pointed it at the Lorenzo brothers.

"The kid then asked, 'What do you think, now?'" Lorenzo said. "I'm looking at my brother, and he's got tears in his eyes, and he reluctantly says, 'Yeah, I'll do it.' We were both scared."

The gang member rode off, and the Lorenzo brothers raced home, vowing to never join that gang. The brothers who'd spend their summer days playing basketball or throwing a football always had the safety of home to escape to. Lorenzo's parents, Dennis and Dorothy, provided a loving home, one their son remembers as being filled with laughter and music. And Dennis, a welder, and Dorothy, a thermostat

Saved Twice

company supervisor, instilled a strong work ethic in their two sons.

"My parents believed in God," Lorenzo said. "But I wouldn't say we were a regular churchgoing family. We'd occasionally go to church on Sunday."

That changed when Lorenzo bumped into a life-changing realization at age 25. Through some friends, he found that being a "good guy" wasn't the only requirement for entrance into heaven.

"After reading the scriptures, I realized that wasn't how you had a relationship with the Lord," Lorenzo said. "When I realized that it took asking Christ to take over my life, to ask for forgiveness of my sins, my life changed."

Lorenzo remembers the date he made that decision like a birthday.

"It was September 10, 1983," he said.

At that time, Lorenzo, a seventh-round draft pick of the Golden State Warriors in 1980, was in his third year of an unexpected five-year NBA career. He played for three teams during his career and averaging 5.9 points and 3.5 assists per game. After playing in the NBA, he played guard for Athletes in Action for seven years, the last four as a player-coach. It was that time as a player-coach that turned his focus from going into youth sports ministry to college coaching.

But basketball seemed like a dead end early in Lorenzo's life. As a sophomore in high school, he was cut from the varsity and junior varsity basketball teams.

"I was a late bloomer," Lorenzo said.

Disheartened, Lorenzo transferred to Pius X Matthias High School, closer to his Compton home. By his senior year, he scored a season-high 27 points in a game, but no college scholarships came his way. He enrolled at Cerritos Community College, which was just seven miles from his home. After surviving the cut, beating out several all-league players, Lorenzo moved into the starting lineup. However,

Saved Twice

he had a setback when he flunked a history class and became academically ineligible for the second half of the season.

It was a hard lesson. Cerritos would lose in a championship game, and Lorenzo would watch from the sideline. Later, Lorenzo learned that his coach refused a request to change the history grade to make his point guard eligible.

"If he had fixed my grade, I would have just gone on and try to beat the system," Lorenzo said. "But I learned from that experience. I never had a problem with eligibility again."

It's also why Lorenzo is such a stickler today for his athletes staying up on their studies.

Eventually, Lorenzo, after a strong sophomore year, was recruited by UNLV, Montana, San Diego State and Washington. He'd become a Husky in 1978, starting for two years. He'd become just the second former Husky player to return to Washington to become the basketball coach.

But Lorenzo wasn't Washington's first choice as coach. He was the fourth choice of then-athletic director Barbara Hedges to replace the fired Bob Bender in the spring of 2002. But pecking order didn't deter Lorenzo, who later said, "Once I knew they wanted me, if I was the 10th choice or the 12th choice, didn't matter to me."

Lorenzo arrived at Washington with a reputation for being a disciplinarian. In three-year stints at Pepperdine (1997-99) and Saint Louis (2000-2002), Lorenzo was a hardworking coach, going from a 6-21 record in his first year at Pepperdine to a 19-13 mark in his last season there.

At each stop, Lorenzo applied discipline equally, ensuring that his rules applied to everyone from the starters to the benchwarmers. That rule was tested during the 2003-04 season, when Washington faced the University of Alabama at Birmingham in the first round of the NCAA tournament. Lorenzo benched starters Will Conroy and Bobby Jones for

Saved Twice

the first four minutes of that game because of minor curfew violations. The Huskies started slowly and lost, 102-100.

Yet Lorenzo doesn't regret his decision to punish the two starters.

"There is a certain way to build a program," Lorenzo said. "Your discipline must be consistent. Players are not dummies. You can't kid a kid. They'll figure out what's important to you and what isn't."

Lorenzo said rules always have to be enforced consistently, no matter what the cost.

"If it comes to the game being on the line and that a players thinks he can do whatever he wants and get away with it, you're in trouble," Lorenzo said. "Then there is slippage. Then you're at the mercy of your guys."

To avoid that tug-of-war, he says, rules have to be enforced regardless of the circumstances.

"Most people take the path of least resistance," Lorenzo said. "Everyone has to understand that from here on, we better do things right."

Lorenzo did that when he first arrived, curbing Doug Wrenn's offensive role and forcing the all-conference guard into a reduced role offensively. Team, not individuals, would be Lorenzo's emphasis.

It had a progressive impact. Washington started 15-25 under Lorenzo, then went 43-9 over the next 52 games. The turnaround was kick-started by the Huskies' remarkable comeback win in 2004 at Oregon State, a game in which Washington rallied from 16 points down in the final seven minutes. It was Washington's first conference win in six games that season.

In the three years prior to Lorenzo's arrival, Washington went 10-20, 10-20 and 11-18.

"Hard work, that's the topic of our discussions," said former Huskies guard Brandon Roy, now with the Portland Trail Blazers. "The only thing we really get in trouble about

Saved Twice

is lack of effort. You can miss shots. You can dribble the ball off your foot. But effort, that's a given."

Lorenzo uses his past, his faith in Christ and a determination to succeed as a compass. He doesn't allow his players to wear their hair in braids or cornrows. Players who show up late to a meeting aren't allowed in. If a player isn't fitting into the offense and is playing one-on-one, he's benched.

His teams don't curse, usually. They don't wear headbands.

Lorenzo's coaching is shaped by his Christian faith, built on discipline, commitment and trust. Discipline is a priority. The word "Bible" doesn't come up. But the principles are used.

"I don't think you can win consistently with bad people in your program," Lorenzo said.

Lorenzo hasn't allowed the success, the fame and the wealth to become a distraction to his Christian faith. He's got other priorities.

"I'm convinced that I'm only in this position because God has placed me here to bring glory to Him," Lorenzo said. "The perspective I have is that the more publicity, the more high profile, the better, because God is going to get the glory."

Lorenzo isn't intimidated by success. Instead, he sees it as an opportunity to put the light not on himself, but on God.

"My background in Athletes in Action helped me understand that God can use anyone," Lorenzo said. "But at the same time, people like to be associated with a winner. That's why, with Athletes in Action, we always tried to put the best athletes out on the floor."

A successful Athletes in Action team would challenge the premise that Christians are "soft and can't compete," Lorenzo said.

Saved Twice

"So, the better we are, the more I can give glory to God," Lorenzo said.

Lorenzo doesn't hide his Christian faith. He closes his answering machine greeting with, "God bless." He openly shares his faith, comparing it to the pride of a newlywed husband.

"A wedding is a celebration," Lorenzo said. "It's not something the grooms wants to be quiet about. He wants everyone to know. He's constantly talking about this lady he loves. So, with the Lord, why does it have to be so secretive?"

He's a sharer of the good news, but he's not a Bible thumper.

"I don't think I'm going to paint my car with scriptures," Lorenzo said. "Or I'm not going to stand on the corner with a megaphone, yelling, 'You're going to burn in hell.' But at the same time, I'm proud of the fact that I have a relationship with the Lord."

Lorenzo said his greatest challenge in his Christian walk is maintaining a balance. He said the concerns that a coach has about recruiting, about how his players are doing in the classroom and personally, about how the team is doing on the court and about that day's practice schedule, can all push in on his day.

"There's so much going on," Lorenzo said. "You're like a CEO. And it preoccupies my thoughts so much, it takes time away from spending time with he Lord like I need to. ... That's my biggest struggle."

But Lorenzo said his own devotions are his best preparation for life's demands and challenges.

"The biggest mentor for me has been the scriptures and the Lord," Lorenzo said. "That has allowed me to mature more than anything. It's taught me discipline, about dealing with people."

And how to turn a perennial loser into a national power at Washington.

Chapter 12

Graduation, Cancer and Chemo

§&

Nobody else was awake. Not her mom, dad or brother. Quietly Sarah Yellenich slipped through her front door and began jogging down the street, the soft patter of her running shoes the only noise as she cut through the still darkness. It's 5:30 a.m. Before school. Before the day's bustle begins.

But with her busy schedule—high school, a part-time job at a grocery store and homework—it was her only chance to squeeze in a workout. During the basketball season it was her fourth-quarter edge on the opponent who slept in. Now, it was just another one of her get-ahead habits.

It was her way of being in control of things.

But a couple of blocks into her jog, a sharp pain in her side forced her to stop.

"What in the heck is that?" she said, rubbing her side.

The pain stopped, and she resumed running, her brown ponytail swinging back and forth.

Twenty minutes later she returned to a kitchen alive with activity. Her mom, a kindergarten teacher, and her dad, a vice principal at the high school she attended, were at the breakfast table along with her younger brother.

Saved Twice

"Good morning, everybody," Sarah said, slipping a piece of bread into the toaster.

Her brother didn't look up from his cereal.

"Mom, I've been having this pain in my side," Sarah said. "I think I hurt it pushing a load of those dumb grocery carts back into the store."

Her toast popped up, and she spread peanut butter across it.

"Well, maybe you should see a doctor," Sarah's mom, Margie, said. "Just to get it checked."

Two more weeks and Sarah would be graduating from high school. She couldn't wait for the all-night party after graduation that her school was sponsoring. A couple of busloads of seniors were headed to Seattle for a night of video games, bowling, eating pizza and just being together for one last time. Sarah had already bought a ticket for $130. She couldn't wait.

"I guess it wouldn't hurt to have a doctor take a look," Sarah said as she took another bite of toast. "It's been bugging me. Do you think it could be a hernia?"

Over the next couple of days the pain intensified. Her stomach began to bloat, and nothing sounded good to eat. Not even pizza. She began skipping meals. She was so bloated she stopped running, ending her four-month stretch of running every day. She began feeling drowsy all the time, occasionally resting her head on her hand in class as she fought to stay awake. Keeping her brown eyes open was an effort.

"Not getting enough sleep, Sarah?" a teacher asked one day as she dozed in class.

That night Margie drove her daughter to the emergency room because of stomach pain. It was the first week of June. The emergency doctor poked her stomach and noticed the obvious swelling. He asked Margie to leave the examination room.

"When was the last time you had sex?" the doctor asked.

77

Saved Twice

Sarah was stunned.

"What do you mean?" she stammered.

"You're pregnant," he said.

"That's not possible," Sarah said. "I've never had sex. That's not something I do."

The doctor examined her pelvis and felt swelling that he decided was a baby. He also noticed a hernia in her side. Surgery was scheduled for Friday, three days after graduation. She told her mom about the surgery, but not about what the doctor said.

"I'll be okay," Sarah said to her mom as they drove home.

A lot of things were swirling through Sarah's head graduation night. Dressed in her green graduation gown, she walked with 270 classmates to receive their diplomas. With all the excitement she barely noticed her stomach pain. She was excited, but she was also exhausted.

"Come on, Sarah," a friend said, grabbing her by the arm. "Let's get on the bus."

"I can't go," Sarah said. "There's no way I could stay awake all night."

It felt strange watching her friends load onto the bus, laughing and carrying on. Sadly Sarah headed for home and went right to bed, leaving her relatives who had come to her house for a graduation party. She felt so rude, but she couldn't keep her eyes open.

"What is the matter with me, God?" Sarah prayed before drifting off to sleep. "Help me, God. I'm out of control."

Three days later Sarah was on the operating table for what was supposed to be a simple procedure. But in addition to a hernia a tumor the size of a softball was found on her left fallopian tube. Four quarts of fluid were drained.

"We're going to have to operate again," a grim-faced doctor, still dressed in his green surgical clothing, told Sarah's parents.

78

Saved Twice

There was dead silence.

"We'll undergo more tests to see if she has any other tumors," the doctor said.

A scan taken the next morning showed the tumor had already increased in size and was now the size of a cantaloupe. But there were no other tumors. The doctor slapped X-rays onto a light table.

He said the lump was cancerous, and it had to come out right away. Surgery was planned in five days.

"For the first time in my life I saw my dad cry," Sarah said.

So many things flashed through her mind when she heard she had cancer. She wondered if she'd ever be married, if she'd ever have children and if she'd live to see her nineteenth birthday.

"It was scary to think this thing inside of me growing incredibly fast could take my life. But I was never afraid of dying. Dying meant going to heaven. I wasn't afraid of that."

Going through the surgery, chemo and pain. Now that scared her.

Three days later Sarah's parents drove her to the University of Washington Hospital, where she'd undergo surgery. Cancer ran in Sarah's family. Her aunt and grandpa both died from colon cancer. Her grandma survived breast cancer. So her parents had already seen cancer up close. Now it had come to take their daughter.

On the morning of surgery, Sarah could barely move she was in so much pain. Her left fallopian tube had ruptured. Before going into surgery Sarah remembers looking up at her parents.

"We're praying for you, Sarah," her mom said, squeezing Sarah's hand.

They wheeled Sarah out and pushed her toward surgery.

Saved Twice

"Funny. I'm always the one in control, planning a school project or an afternoon outing with friends," she said. "Now I was merely the helpless bystander."

So this was how fast you could go. This was how fast life could change. There was no controlling it.

During a three-and-a-half-hour surgery doctors opened an eight-inch incision, cutting out a tumor the size of a volleyball. It had nearly doubled in size in just five days. It was an aggressively growing cancer that had first appeared four weeks earlier in mid May, raising questions about Sarah's chances and whether or not it had spread. As a precaution Sarah's appendix and lymph nodes in her legs were also removed.

The tumor was out, but a question remained. What kind of cancer was it? Ovarian, which had a fifteen-percent chance of recovery if caught late? Or was it a germ cell tumor, which had a ninety-percent recovery rate? For a week the Yellenich family nervously waited for the results, wondering, fretting and praying.

"On my parents' wedding anniversary I sat between my mom and dad in the doctor's office, clutching their hands as we braced for the news," Sarah said.

The doctor's smile as he entered the room gave them their answer.

"You've got a great chance of beating this."

Sarah had a germ cell tumor. It was as if they'd won a championship game.

"We hugged and cried," Sarah said. "What a relief. I was going to live."

But not before she experienced the hardest six weeks of her life. She had to go through chemotherapy.

"Chemotherapy didn't kill me, but it took me right to the edge," Sarah said.

Because of the aggressive nature of her cancer her doctor opted for an aggressive attack. Chemo treatments were

Saved Twice

spread over a six-week span, rather than five or six months. It was intense, demanding and extremely nauseating.

Her life became one long IV drip. She'd check into the hospital for three days and was strapped up to the IV that pumped chemo through her body, burning through her veins. She received three mega doses two weeks apart. In between injections she had a mini chemo dose.

For eight hours after the big doses Sarah vomited nearly nonstop. Nurses brought her a tray with broth and jello.

"At first I'd try to eat, and I'd puke. It was awful," Sarah said. "Even the sight of food made me sick."

By then she weighed one hundred pounds, thirty less than she did during basketball when she made first-team all-league as a forward. She was skin and bones. Still, food was the curse.

"Please, can you take that away?" Sarah would tell the nurse, retching at the smell of food.

"I wasn't the most patient patient," she admitted.

By the third day after treatment she could eat, which always signaled her release from the hospital. And when she'd walk out of the hospital, with her mom and dad at her sides supporting her, it was as if the world suddenly switched from black and white to color. Stepping outside was simply amazing.

"Look at the blue sky," she'd say as if she were seeing it for the first time.

Her hair came out in patches. Soon she was completely bald. Losing her hair was like losing her identity. She wore a wig for a while, but that wasn't who she was. She decided she was being phony. She wore bandannas instead.

"What do you think, Mom?" she'd ask, tugging on a red bandanna.

"You look great," her mom said.

Slowly Sarah's hair returned. When she could actually comb it over, she stopped wearing a bandanna.

Saved Twice

"People told me how cute my haircut was," Sarah said. "I wanted to say it was an eighty-thousand-dollar haircut, but I didn't."

In September doctors took a hundred biopsies to check for any signs of cancer. They also ended up taking a small piece of her colon to remove a tumor fried by chemo. Again she sat in the doctor's office, sandwiched between her parents, waiting for a report.

"You are cancer free," he said.

A squeeze by her parents never felt so good.

"When cancer strikes you lose all dignity," Sarah said. "You lose this feeling of invincibility. And when you hear you're a survivor, a lucky one, you gain this incredible sense of appreciation for the now, for family and for friends."

The nausea was the chemo working. The peace was God working.

"This may sound crazy, but cancer is the best thing that's ever happened to me," Sarah said. "I hated going through it. But I love what it's done to me."

All the things that meant so much: combed hair, the right outfit, fitting in and being in control. That's not Sarah's compass anymore.

"I'm not so consumed with how I look. Being with my family, sitting around watching TV on a Friday night or going to church with them on Sunday—those are the things that mean so much now."

Facing death is the ultimate lie detector. You find out what's really important, what you really believe. And you find out you're never really in control.

"I'm okay with that. Being in control is God's job," Sarah said.

Chapter 13

A Race Against Death

"Push yourself," a determined John Olerud thought as he ran around the track.

A throbbing headache had returned. But thinking his headache came only because he was out of shape, Olerud ran harder, going stride for stride with a teammate on the Washington State University baseball team.

Then Olerud collapsed. A race for life began.

"I was scared," he said. "I didn't know what was going on."

Unknowingly, a time bomb had been ticking in his head.

In January 1989, Olerud collapsed while working out his junior year at Washington State, nearly dying from an aneurysm at the base of his brain. He had complained of headaches during fall workouts, but dismissed them as nothing more than being out of shape.

He was 20 years old, seemingly with the world by the tail after batting .464 and going 15-0 as a pitcher the previous season. Then he suffered a grand mal seizure when a blood vein in the back of his head nearly ruptured.

"That showed me that I'm not in as much control of things as I thought I was," Olerud said.

Saved Twice

After collapsing, Olerud stayed in the hospital two weeks as doctors ran tests trying to find the aneurysm. When they couldn't, they released him.

Several weeks later, Olerud, at the suggestion of his father, who is a doctor, underwent further tests at the University of Washington hospital. It was there that his aneurysm was discovered. He underwent a risky surgery procedure Feb. 27 and played his first game April 15, wearing a batter's helmet at the plate and in the field to protect the incision. Wearing a helmet in the field became Olerud's trademark throughout his pro career while playing for the Toronto Blue Jays, New York Mets, Seattle Mariners, New York Yankees and Boston Red Sox.

"It is a miracle," Olerud said about his recovery from surgery. "No question. I've seen children in rehab wards trying to recover from surgery like mind. And it wasn't as easy."

His recovery was remarkable. There was no rehabilitation. No learning to walk again. No learning to talk again. Those were all the things doctor told Olerud he'd likely face. He returned to baseball that spring and ended up being named college's player of the year.

His brush with death didn't slow him a bit.

"God spared me so I can have an input on somebody else," Olerud said. "He spared me so that I would be able to glorify his name with my life. Hopefully, just talking about Him and telling others what He's meant to my life will encourage other people to seek Him out."

A friend once described Olerud as being "just north of comatose." Mild, calm and collect.

That's John Olerud, the former major league all-star first baseman with a career .295 battling average over 17 seasons.

He's nicknamed Big Rude. But actually, he's more Mister Rogers. The worst thing written about Olerud is he's a big

Saved Twice

eater. He memorized the menu for the locker rooms of every major league baseball park. He could tell you that Anaheim's got chili with onions, Detroit has sandwiches made to order, Baltimore has spicy crabs and Cleveland is big on finger food.

"I guess you could say I like to eat," the slender 6-foot-5, 220-pound Olerud said.

Rarely was he seen without food in his hand while boarding a team bus. Rarer yet is a moment when Olerud blows his cool on the field or in the locker room. That's what made Olerud's arguing an umpire's decision so surprising that a Seattle reporter wrote about it. After being called out on strikes for the third time by umpire Dale Scott in a game against Texas, Olerud barked about the call. It was an uncharacteristic outburst.

"I've always had this real calm demeanor," Olerud said. "That doesn't mean I'm not getting wound up or I'm not feeling butterflies. I just don't show it."

But what's to get riled about? It's been a wonderful life for John Olerud.

Olerud became just the 17th player to go directly into the major leagues after the Toronto Blue Jays drafted him in the third round in 1989. He won two World Series rings while with Toronto, been to the playoffs six times on three different teams and married his high school sweetheart. He played a game he loves and was paid millions. Making $7.7 million in his final season with the Seattle Mariners, he made more money than he ever dream of spending. He has an adoring family, and he can eat whatever he wants and never gain a pound.

"No question, I've been blessed," he said.

Yet all isn't perfect.

First came the grand mal seizure.

Then in August 2000, that message about not having control over life was repeated. Olerud's second child, Jordan,

Saved Twice

was born missing one chromosome and part of another, resulting in her inability to eat, walk or talk. Doctors haven't found any other illness like it in the country. At 2 years of age, Jordan couldn't roll over on her own.

Naturally, Olerud's response was "Why God?"

He got his answer one afternoon when he was holding Jordan while a nurse stuck a needle in her arm to begin an IV for a feeding.

"I was looking down at my daughter," Olerud said. "She's getting poked. Here she was in what she thought were safe hands. And I'm letting them poke her."

Olerud wanted to explain to his daughter what was happening. But any explanation wouldn't be understood.

"I think a lot of times as Christians we think, 'God what's going on?'" Olerud said. "If you're there, why are you letting me get poked? Just like my daughter, we often don't understand what's going on. We pray 'Do something about this.' And I'm sure God is up there saying, 'Love to explain it to you, but you wouldn't understand. Trust me.'"

Olerud said there are no messages in the Bible about guaranteed prosperity for Christians. There are no guarantees about a life without trials or hardships if you become a Christian.

"The first chapter of James has been a big help for me," Olerud said. "God uses trials to make us more mature and complete. That's part of our growing. Ultimately, there is going to be prosperity when we get to heaven. It's going to be unbelievable."

Problems come. Even for Christians. Olerud's plan was to have healthy kids. His plan was to get married, have children and live happily ever after. A life with no problems. No frets. No hardships. After all, he was a Christian.

"If you're thinking you're going to get everything you want in life because you're a Christian, you're going to sour

86

Saved Twice

on Christianity," Olerud said. "Because there are going to be trials."

When he was in college, Olerud's understanding of what it meant to be a Christian was superficial. While raised in a Christian home, he missed the point.

"When I was a kid, I asked my parents one day what religion we were," Olerud said. "They told me we were Christians. So, I thought I was a Christian. I didn't realize that was a decision I had to make myself. It wasn't a decision my parents made for me."

It was Kelly, while they were dating and before they were married, who got Olerud to understand what it meant to be a Christian.

"She asked me all these questions and got me reading the Bible," he said. "It was then that I realized that I had to accept Christ as my Lord and Savior."

Olerud had a successful career. He won a batting title in 1993, hitting over .400 through August that year and finishing at .363. He was a two-time All-Star and a three-time Gold Glove.

Throughout his career, Olerud was unflappable.

"It's like he doesn't have any sweat glands," former Mariner manager Bob Melvin said.

Wherever he's gone, Olerud has been the calming influence in a locker room, helping Toronto and the New York Mets reach the World Series. With the Mariners, he reached the American League championship twice.

Olerud retired from baseball in 2005 after 17 years in the major leagues. He was a picture of consistency throughout his career, collecting 2,239 hits in 2,234 games while playing for five teams. With the Mets, he set single-season team records for batting average (.354), on-base percentage (.447), most walks (125) and times on base (309).

Yet success, money and fame haven't gone to his head. He's not overly unimpressed with himself. The player team-

Saved Twice

mates call Big Rude, which is a shorter version of his last name rather than a reflection of his character, is known as Mr. Nice Guy around the league.

He said he's just someone striving to grow in his Christian faith.

"Christ is going to be the one working on me," he said. "He's going to be the one doing the perfecting. That's a good thing, too."

That's because the guy with the reputation for being perfect knows he's not.

LaVergne, TN USA
11 May 2010
182298LV00003B/189/P